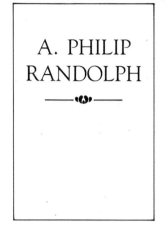

A. PHILIP
RANDOLPH

A. PHILIP RANDOLPH

Sally Hanley

Senior Consulting Editor
Nathan Irvin Huggins
Director
W.E.B. Du Bois Institute for Afro-American Research
Harvard University

CHELSEA HOUSE PUBLISHERS

New York   Philadelphia

Chelsea House Publishers

Editor-in-Chief   Nancy Toff
Executive Editor   Remmel T. Nunn
Managing Editor   Karyn Gullen Browne
Copy Chief   Juliann Barbato
Picture Editor   Adrian G. Allen
Art Director   Maria Epes
Manufacturing Manager   Gerald Levine

Black Americans of Achievement

Senior Editor   Richard Rennert

Staff for A. PHILIP RANDOLPH

Associate Editor   Perry King
Assistant Editor   Gillian Bucky
Copy Editor   Karen Hammonds
Deputy Copy Chief   Ellen Scordato
Editorial Assistant   Susan DeRosa
Picture Researcher   Alan Gottlieb
Assistant Art Director   Laurie Jewell
Design Assistant   Laura Lang
Production Coordinator   Joseph Romano
Cover Illustration   Alan J. Nahigian

7 9 8 6

Library of Congress Cataloging-in-Publication Data

Hanley, Sally.
    A. Philip Randolph.

    (Black Americans of achievement)
    Bibliography: p.
    Includes index.
    Summary: A biography of the civil rights activist who or-
ganized the Brotherhood of Sleeping Car Porters, which acted
as a labor union for Pullman car porters.
    1. Randolph, A. Philip (Asa Philip), 1889–   —Juvenile
literature.   2. Afro-Americans—Biography—Juvenile literature.   3. Afro-Americans—Civil rights—Juvenile literature.
[1. Randolph, A. Philip (Asa Philip), 1889–   .   2. Civil
rights workers.   2. Afro-Americans—Biography]
I. Title.   II. Series.
E185.97R27H36   1988   323.4′092′4 [92]   87-34118
ISBN 1-55546-607-9
       0-7910-0222-5   (pbk.)

CONTENTS

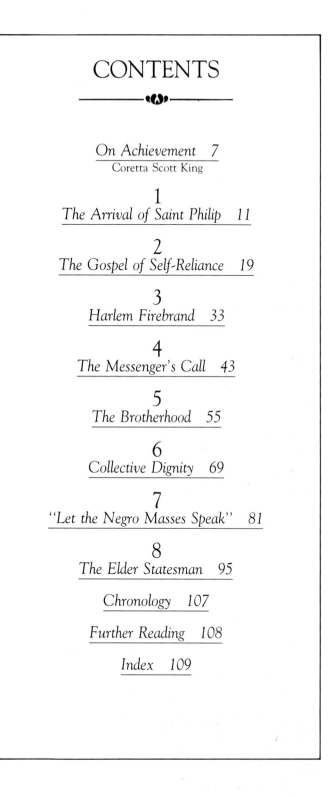

BLACK AMERICANS OF ACHIEVEMENT

RALPH ABERNATHY
civil rights leader

MUHAMMAD ALI
heavyweight champion

RICHARD ALLEN
religious leader and social activist

LOUIS ARMSTRONG
musician

ARTHUR ASHE
tennis great

JOSEPHINE BAKER
entertainer

JAMES BALDWIN
author

BENJAMIN BANNEKER
scientist and mathematician

AMIRI BARAKA
poet and playwright

COUNT BASIE
bandleader and composer

ROMARE BEARDEN
artist

JAMES BECKWOURTH
frontiersman

MARY MCLEOD
BETHUNE
educator

BLANCHE BRUCE
politician

RALPH BUNCHE
diplomat

GEORGE WASHINGTON
CARVER
botanist

CHARLES CHESNUTT
author

BILL COSBY
entertainer

PAUL CUFFE
merchant and abolitionist

FATHER DIVINE
religious leader

FREDERICK DOUGLASS
abolitionist editor

CHARLES DREW
physician

W.E.B. DU BOIS
scholar and activist

PAUL LAURENCE DUNBAR
poet

KATHERINE DUNHAM
dancer and choreographer

MARIAN WRIGHT EDELMAN
civil rights leader and lawyer

DUKE ELLINGTON
bandleader and composer

RALPH ELLISON
author

JULIUS ERVING
basketball great

JAMES FARMER
civil rights leader

ELLA FITZGERALD
singer

MARCUS GARVEY
black-nationalist leader

DIZZY GILLESPIE
musician

PRINCE HALL
social reformer

W. C. HANDY
father of the blues

WILLIAM HASTIE
educator and politician

MATTHEW HENSON
explorer

CHESTER HIMES
author

BILLIE HOLIDAY
singer

JOHN HOPE
educator

LENA HORNE
entertainer

LANGSTON HUGHES
poet

ZORA NEALE HURSTON
author

JESSE JACKSON
civil rights leader and politician

JACK JOHNSON
heavyweight champion

JAMES WELDON JOHNSON
author

SCOTT JOPLIN
composer

BARBARA JORDAN
politician

MARTIN LUTHER KING, JR.
civil rights leader

ALAIN LOCKE
scholar and educator

JOE LOUIS
heavyweight champion

RONALD MCNAIR
astronaut

MALCOLM X
militant black leader

THURGOOD MARSHALL
Supreme Court justice

ELIJAH MUHAMMAD
religious leader

JESSE OWENS
champion athlete

CHARLIE PARKER
musician

GORDON PARKS
photographer

SIDNEY POITIER
actor

ADAM CLAYTON POWELL, JR.
political leader

LEONTYNE PRICE
opera singer

A. PHILIP RANDOLPH
labor leader

PAUL ROBESON
singer and actor

JACKIE ROBINSON
baseball great

BILL RUSSELL
basketball great

JOHN RUSSWURM
publisher

SOJOURNER TRUTH
antislavery activist

HARRIET TUBMAN
antislavery activist

NAT TURNER
slave revolt leader

DENMARK VESEY
slave revolt leader

MADAM C. J. WALKER
entrepreneur

BOOKER T. WASHINGTON
educator

HAROLD WASHINGTON
politician

WALTER WHITE
civil rights leader and author

RICHARD WRIGHT
author

ON
ACHIEVEMENT

Coretta Scott King

Before you begin this book, I hope you will ask yourself what the word excellence means to you. I think that it's a question we should all ask, and keep asking as we grow older and change. Because the truest answer to it should never change. When you think of excellence, perhaps you think of success at work; or of becoming wealthy; or meeting the right person, getting married, and having a good family life.

Those important goals are worth striving for, but there is a better way to look at excellence. As Martin Luther King, Jr., said in one of his last sermons, "I want you to be first in love. I want you to be first in moral excellence. I want you to be first in generosity. If you want to be important, wonderful. If you want to be great, wonderful. But recognize that he who is greatest among you shall be your servant."

My husband, Martin Luther King, Jr., knew that the true meaning of achievement is service. When I met him, in 1952, he was already ordained as a Baptist preacher and was working towards a doctoral degree at Boston University. I was studying at the New England Conservatory and dreamed of accomplishments in music. We married a year later, and after I graduated the following year we moved to Montgomery, Alabama. We didn't know it then, but our notions of achievement were about to undergo a dramatic change.

You may have read or heard about what happened next. What began with the boycott of a local bus line grew into a national movement, and by the time he was assassinated in 1968 my husband had fashioned a black movement powerful enough to shatter forever the practice of racial segregation. What you may not have read about is where he got his method for resisting injustice without compromising his religious beliefs.

He got the strategy of nonviolence from a man of a different race, who lived in a distant country, and even practiced a different religion. The man was Mahatma Gandhi, the great leader of India, who devoted his life to serving humanity in the spirit of love and nonviolence. It was in these principles that Martin discovered his method for social reform. More than anything else, those two principles were the key to his achievements.

This book is about black Americans who served society through the excellence of their achievements. It forms a part of the rich history of black men and women in America—a history of stunning accomplishments in every field of human endeavor, from literature and art to science, industry, education, diplomacy, athletics, jurisprudence, even polar exploration.

Not all of the people in this history had the same ideals, but I think you will find something that all of them have in common. Like Martin Luther King, Jr., they all decided to become "drum majors" and serve humanity. In that principle—whether it was expressed in books, inventions, or song—they found something outside themselves to use as a goal and a guide. Something that showed them a way to serve others, instead of living only for themselves.

Reading the stories of these courageous men and women not only helps us discover the principles that we will use to guide our own lives, but it teaches us about our black heritage and about America itself. It is crucial for us to know the heroes and heroines of our history and to realize that the price we paid in our struggle for equality in America was dear. But we must also understand that we have gotten as far as we have partly because America's democratic system and ideals made it possible.

We still are struggling with racism and prejudice. But the great men and women in this series are a tribute to the spirit of our democratic ideals and the system in which they have flourished. And that makes their stories special, and worth knowing. ◆

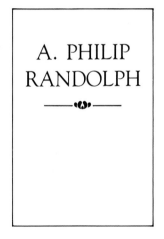

A. PHILIP RANDOLPH

1

THE ARRIVAL
OF
SAINT PHILIP

❦

ON THE EVENING of June 16, 1942, the huge arena of Madison Square Garden in New York City was filled with more than 20,000 black Americans. They were eagerly taking part in a giant rally as an expression of black solidarity attended by the leading civil rights leaders of the day. However, the audience was still awaiting the arrival of the person who was responsible for fostering the massive event. Then 100 men in uniform strode to the center of the arena, flanking a tall, straight-backed man.

Suddenly, sections of the crowd started to cheer. More and more of them began to realize that the uniformed men were members of the Brotherhood of Sleeping Car Porters, a union of black workers—and that the person whom they were escorting was Asa Philip Randolph. Having organized the union nearly 30 years before, he was now, at the age of 53, sometimes called "Saint Philip of the Pullman Porters."

The Brotherhood of Sleeping Car Porters had been formed by Randolph to unite the nation's porters in their fight for better working conditions. The porters were all employees of the Pullman Palace Car Company, a sleeping-car railroad company that by the early 20th century had become one of the largest

Randolph rose to national prominence after organizing the nation's first trade union for black workers. Five years later, more than 20,000 people answered his call for a demonstration of black unity at Madison Square Garden in New York City.

11

Randolph formed the March on Washington Movement (MOWM) to marshal support for integrating the armed forces and defense industries. He told black audiences, "You possess power, great power," but warned them that "nothing counts but pressure, more pressure, and still more pressure."

employers of black labor in America. The working agreement that Randolph and the Brotherhood eventually reached with the Pullman Company—after years of contention—was the first labor pact ever signed between a group of black workers and a large American corporation.

The signing of this historic labor agreement in 1937 proved to be more than just a long and hard-fought victory for the Brotherhood. It also encouraged Randolph to take a leading role in the fight for civil rights, especially when racism in the nation's military establishment was becoming increasingly evident as World War II drew near. "There was no other group of Negroes in America who constituted the key to unlocking the door of a nationwide struggle for Negro rights as the porters," he maintained.

As the United States prepared itself for World War II, the American people united against Nazi Germany and Fascist Italy—countries that had become enemies of democracy and human rights. Yet the war effort also exposed deep divisions within American society. The United States government maintained a segregated military and supported discriminatory hiring practices in defense industry jobs. Randolph and other civil rights leaders had been decrying such racism in the armed forces and the defense industry since the days of World War I.

With the support of his loyal network of porters, Randolph began to put pressure on President Franklin Roosevelt in 1940, asking his administration to correct the injustice of having blacks fight for their country but only as second-class citizens. When Randolph's pleas met with refusals, he hit upon one of the most historic forms of protest in America. He called for "a thundering march on Washington."

The march on the nation's capital would consist only of blacks. They would sit on the White House lawn until they were given equal treatment in the

In June 1941, Randolph persuaded President Franklin Roosevelt to issue an executive order banning racial discrimination in the defense industries. However, he was unable to persuade the president that black soldiers (such as this army paratrooper) should not be forced to serve in segregated units.

military and jobs in the defense industry. According to Lester Granger, the executive director of the National Urban League (an equal opportunity agency for minorities), "It was Randolph's immense prestige among all classes of Negroes that made this idea something more than a pretentious notion."

Randolph's threat of the March on Washington Movement (MOWM) encouraged President Roosevelt to appoint a Fair Employment Practices Committee in 1941 to look into complaints of discrimination concerning the employment of workers. The New York *Amsterdam News*, a leading black newspaper, subsequently remarked that Randolph "is ranked along with the great Frederick Douglass. His name is rapidly becoming a household word." However, Randolph knew that his work of gaining equal rights for blacks was far from finished. Consequently, he proposed that the March on Washington Movement broaden its efforts in its attempt to wipe out racism.

In the midst of the expansion of the March on Washington Movement, the political climate in America shifted. The Japanese bombed Pearl Harbor on December 7, 1941, and brought America into the war in the Pacific. Some of the driving force of the movement against racism drained away as the nation's attention turned toward this new development.

America's black leaders realized the effect that total immersion in a war would have on civil rights progress. Walter White, the secretary of the National Association for the Advancement of Colored People (NAACP), expressed the fear of many of these leaders by saying, "Declarations of war do not lessen the obligation to preserve and extend civil liberties here while the fight is being made to restore freedom from dictatorship abroad." Consequently, Randolph and representatives of the March on Washington Move-

After the Japanese bombed the American naval base at Pearl Harbor, Hawaii, on December 7, 1941, the United States declared war on Japan and its allies, Germany and Italy. Although a firm pacifist, Randolph supported the war—especially against German dictator Adolf Hitler's racist Nazi regime.

Walter White, secretary of the National Association for the Advancement of Colored People, believed—as did Randolph—that the struggle against racism in America must be pursued even during wartime.

ment announced that they were initiating a campaign of civil disobedience, a political tactic of nonviolent obstruction that was devised by Hindu nationalist leader Mahatma Gandhi, who had fought against racism and British imperialism in India.

Randolph planned a series of giant rallies to gather support for this campaign. The first was to be held in Madison Square Garden. It was to be followed by others in Chicago, Illinois, and St. Louis, Missouri. Randolph insisted, "Our aim then must not only be to defeat Nazism, Fascism, and militarism on the battlefield but to win the peace for democracy, for freedom, and the Brotherhood of Man without regard to his pigmentation." By making these plans, he indicated that blacks would not keep silent on the issue of color—not even in the name of patriotism.

Always an inspiring and eloquent speaker, Randolph urged blacks to organize and demand their full rights as American citizens. He pointed out that "you get what you can take, and you keep what you can hold," but "you can't take anything without organization."

The demonstration preparations went ahead. Meetings were funded by the Brotherhood of Sleeping Car Porters, whose nationwide membership was instrumental in the planning. Randolph took to the street corners of Harlem, the New York district that had become the black capital of America, and gave speeches while standing on the top of a soapbox. With the area around him decked out with flags and posters, he handed out leaflets exhorting the black population to come to Madison Square Garden on the evening of June 16, 1942. "Wake up Negro America!" he said. "Do you want work? Do you want equal rights? Do you want justice? Then prepare to fight for it! 50,000 Negroes must storm the Garden. Mobilize now!"

Randolph proposed that a blackout coincide with the New York rally. All American cities were then used to blackouts as part of their civil defense in preparation for possible enemy attacks. The March on Washington Movement called for all night classes, shops, taverns, churches, and other institutions to be shut down on the evening of June 16. For 15 minutes, Harlem would be "dark, silent, and dry," according to Randolph.

The rally took place at Madison Square Garden as scheduled, and it lasted for five hours. Randolph described it as "the biggest demonstration of Negroes in the history of the world." The chief personality of the evening, he was applauded for the incredible impact he had made on the lives of all black Americans. Murray Kempton, one of the nation's leading journalists, explained this impact on American society by saying, "It is hard to make anyone who has never met him believe that A. Philip Randolph must be the greatest man who has lived in the United States in this century. But it is harder yet to make anyone who has ever known him believe anything else."

For decades to come, Randolph would continue to play a leading role in the civil rights and trade-union movements. Deeply committed to his principles, he never sacrificed the reputation for integrity and loyalty that enabled him to shape a better society not just for the Brotherhood and for blacks but for all Americans.

2
THE GOSPEL
OF
SELF-RELIANCE

ASA PHILIP RANDOLPH was born on April 15, 1889, in Crescent City, Florida. He was the son of poor but upstanding and proud parents. His beliefs and character were shaped from birth by his devoutly religious family and the strongly knit black community in which he was raised.

Asa spent most of his youth in Jacksonville, Florida, which was a vigorous and thriving business center in the 1890s. Located on the St. Johns River in the northeastern corner of Florida, the town was a port through which flowed the products of the local farms and lumber mills. It was also a popular winter resort for northerners.

During Asa's youth, Jacksonville was one of the most integrated towns in the South. Blacks made up one third of the town's population and lived in racially mixed communities. They held positions of responsibility as policemen, city councilmen, justices of the peace, and judges of the municipal court. Although there were separate schools for blacks and whites in Jacksonville, the black children who lived there had the opportunity to attain higher education—unlike most black children in the South. Thus, when Asa was growing up, he did not encounter the

Randolph grew up in the prosperous port of Jacksonville, Florida. The city's handsome downtown commercial district is shown here.

19

rigid segregation and racial oppression that existed elsewhere in much of the South. Not only did he see blacks in positions of authority, but he also had a very strong role model in his father.

The Reverend James William Randolph was born in 1864—one year before the end of the Civil War. He was a descendant of slaves who had been owned by the prominent Randolph family of Virginia. While growing up in Monticello, Florida, he had been educated at a grade school founded by northern white missionaries who belonged to the Methodist church. The elder Randolph was trained to be a tailor, but he also felt a strong religious calling and studied the Bible in his spare time. By the time he was 20 years old, he was already ordained as a minister in the African Methodist Episcopal (AME) church.

When the Reverend Randolph became an AME preacher, he joined a long line of black clergymen who had struggled to win freedom and equality for their people. Established in Philadelphia, Pennsylvania, in 1794 by the black religious and social leader Richard Allen, the AME church had been a platform for racial protest for nearly a century. Before the Civil War, the church had been banned in many parts of the South because it was believed that AME preachers were stirring up slave revolts, such as the one led by Denmark Vesey in South Carolina in 1822. In the Reconstruction era that followed the Civil War, Northern troops enforced the civil liberties that Congress had just granted to blacks, and new AME congregations sprang up in Florida and other southern states. The church's publications, *The Christian Recorder* and *The AME Review,* encouraged blacks to be self-reliant and to aggressively defend their newly won freedom. Consequently, these papers were considered dangerously radical by former slaveholders and other conservative southerners.

After being ordained in the AME church, the Reverend Randolph began preaching to the small black community in Baldwin, Florida. There, in 1885, he married Elizabeth Robinson, who was a devout member of his congregation. In 1887, the Randolphs had their first son, James William, Jr. Two years later, after the Reverend Randolph took over the congregation in Crescent City, a second son was born. He was named Asa after the biblical ruler who rid his kingdom of foreign idols and gave up his wealth to save his country from invaders.

When Asa was two years old, his father decided to accept an invitation to become the minister of a small congregation in Jacksonville that met on Sundays in a rented room. To supplement his meager income, the Reverend Randolph also preached in black farm communities around Jacksonville, earning a few coins or a sack of potatoes for his efforts. As Asa and his brother grew older, they began to accompany their father on his travels, which sometimes

Randolph received a strong religious upbringing from his father, who was an African Methodist Episcopal (AME) preacher. When Randolph grew older, he sometimes went to hear the eloquent sermons given by the minister of the Bethel Baptist Church (shown here) in Jacksonville.

Jacksonville, Fla. Bethel Baptist Institutional Church

involved a 50-mile trip upriver and a taxing journey through swamps and over rough country trails. The tall, handsome, gentlemanly preacher was popular with his congregations. He taught what Asa later described as a "racial religion," and his sermons emphasized the AME belief in the need for social reform and equality of the races. The prayer meetings usually included demonstrations of religious ecstasy, with members of the congregation throwing themselves on the ground and testifying to their deep spiritual faith.

Asa grew up in a sparsely furnished rented house in the toughest section of Jacksonville. In the back-yard garden, the family grew bananas, lemons, and collard greens and raised chickens and hogs. The

Jacksonville was known for its relatively liberal racial climate. Black social clubs and integrated organizations such as this brick-layers' union played an important part in community affairs.

home-grown items were a necessity because the Randolphs were constantly in debt. The family could not survive on what the Reverend Randolph earned preaching, so Asa's parents cleaned clothes and did sewing and tailoring work as well. The reverend also started a meat market and firewood business, both of which quickly failed and left him with large bills to pay. Although the kind-hearted reverend was greatly respected within the community, he was a poor businessman and let customers buy on credit. Only Elizabeth Randolph's firm policy of "no money, no clothes" saved the family from desperate straits.

Asa inherited his father's disinterest in accumulating wealth, but he was also strongly influenced by other teachings that the reverend carried from the pulpit into the home. The senior James Randolph instructed his sons to be proud and independent, to stand up to racial discrimination, to be humble but firm in their convictions, and to maintain an erect posture and speak with eloquence and clarity. He also taught them to help the needy and to take on the responsibility of leading others.

The Randolph brothers saw their father as a man who could get things done. An example of his initiative occurred when he organized a sale of fried chicken and fish as part of a fund-raising drive so that his congregation could buy a church building. The brothers also saw their father as a man of courage. Once, when a group of Jacksonville's white residents were threatening to break into the local jail and lynch a black man who was being held there, the reverend and a few friends armed themselves and stood guard outside the jail until tensions cooled down. Elizabeth Randolph sat at home with a shotgun and protected the family while her husband kept his perilous vigil. This small victory over racial oppression was a very important one to Asa. He was taught by his parents not to bow down to racism; he was raised to fight.

Randolph idolized his older brother, James (shown here), an excellent student who fearlessly stood up for his rights.

The fire that devastated Jackson-
ville in 1901 also caused a sharp
rise in racial tensions. Many
black residents believed that the
white members of the fire depart-
ment had not made much of an
effort to save the homes of blacks
from the flames.

Racial discrimination and violence became an ever more visible presence in Asa's life as he grew older. A disastrous fire that burned down much of Jacksonville in 1901 heightened tensions between the races after bands of homeless blacks were accused of looting. The relatively liberal racial atmosphere that existed in his hometown in his early years began to be replaced as the discriminatory Jim Crow laws passed by southern state and municipal legislatures kept blacks from voting, holding government positions, and using the same public facilities as whites. In the early 1900s, Jacksonville's black citizens were deprived of the positions of authority they once held and were forced to use specially marked areas of the town library and public transportation streetcars.

The Reverend Randolph forbade his sons from using the library's segregated reading room or riding on the streetcars, fearing that the use of such facilities would rob them of their self-respect. Because they could not ride on the streetcars, the Randolph brothers had to walk the long distance to the local elementary school where they began their formal education. This was not an easy rule for the Reverend Randolph to impose on his sons. He had spent a great deal of time and energy educating himself, and he wanted to make sure that his sons would not face any barriers that would keep them from acquiring liberal educations, well-read minds, and well-behaved manners.

The Reverend Randolph supplemented his sons' formal schooling with home instruction. Every afternoon, he made Asa and James, Jr., read from the family's small collection of works by William Shakespeare, Charles Dickens, Jane Austen, and other popular writers. The lessons also included a smattering

During Randolph's youth, racial segregation became increasingly enforced throughout the South. Randolph's father forbade his sons from using any segregated public facilities, including the "colored waiting room" in the Jacksonville train station.

While attending the Cookman Institute in Jacksonville, Randolph received especially strong guidance from teachers Lillie Whitney (above) and Mary Neff (on opposite page). Both teachers encouraged him to excel in many different fields.

of American history, church history, and African history. The boys also read articles about social issues in the AME church's publications and a politically radical journal called *The Voice of the Negro.*

The Randolph brothers needed little encouragement to read. It seemed to other children in the neighborhood that the two boys always had their heads buried in books and that they always had the right answers in the classroom. Their stellar performances as students got them into trouble with class bullies, who constantly picked fights with the boys outside the school. James Randolph, Jr., usually stood up to his antagonists, and although Asa disliked using his fists to settle arguments, he always backed up his older brother. When they came home with their lumps and bruises, their mother would ask them if they had defended themselves. If they had not, she would tell them that they should have fought back.

While in elementary school, Asa followed in the footsteps of his brother, with whom he was very close. The academic abilities of both boys were soon apparent to school administrators. In 1903, when Asa was 14 years old, he and James were accepted into Jacksonville's Cookman Institute. The school was one of several black schools established in the post–Civil War South by Methodist missionaries, and it did not charge any tuition. Cookman offered both college-preparatory and trade-oriented courses—a necessary combination for students who would find jobs as plumbers and carpenters more available than those as lawyers and doctors. The curriculum included courses in the sciences, Latin, philosophy, and other liberal arts subjects in addition to such vocational courses as shoemaking, agriculture, and home economics.

At the Cookman Institute, Asa emerged from his brother's shadow and developed his own interests. Encouraged by Mary Neff and Lillie Whitney, two teachers who took a special interest in him, he began to excel in his literature, drama, and public-speaking courses. He was also the best singer in the school choir and the star of its baseball team. Other students respected the soft-spoken, thoughtful young man and looked to him as a leader. When he and his brother graduated from Cookman in 1907, it was he who finished at the top of his class and gave the valedictory address, a speech about the importance of racial pride.

The Randolph brothers were better students than many of the Cookman graduates who went on to college, but for them there was no family money available for higher education. After graduation, they looked for jobs instead. Asa found many and quit many. He collected payments for an insurance company, sold groceries, ran deliveries for a drugstore, stacked logs, did construction work for a railroad company, and shoveled fertilizer. While working at these jobs, he maintained his reading regimen. He also joined a black amateur dramatic group in Jacksonville, and his acting skills and deep baritone voice became noted around town. He began to think about joining a professional theater group, although he knew that the acting profession was not considered respectable enough for a minister's son.

By the time Asa was in his late teens, he had grown to a height of well over six feet, and his thin, bony frame had earned him the nickname String Bean. He was a bit of a dandy and was very careful about his dress and appearance. But behind the stylish clothes and the sly comments he would make to reveal his humorous side, there was a young man who was struggling to find his calling.

Asa knew that he did not want to be a minister like his father. He preferred to read Shakespeare's plays or the poetry of the renowned black writer Paul Laurence Dunbar to reading the Bible. He was distressed that he did not share his parents' intense spiritual faith, but he also found it upsetting to have to

Educator Booker T. Washington (bottom row, at left) was the most powerful black leader in the United States in the early 1900s. He is shown here with a group of teachers from the Tuskegee Institute, the black vocational college in Alabama that he founded in 1881.

pretend to hold the religious convictions expected of a preacher's son. Only reluctantly did his father give up his hopes that Asa would enter the ministry.

Although Asa had no strong religious feelings, he respected the church for the part it played in uniting the black community and preserving its traditions. His childhood heroes had been men such as Henry McNeal Turner, the fearless AME bishop and black nationalist leader who had always carried pistols to defend himself against white racists. Having absorbed the militant racial teachings of the AME church, Asa had resolved to fight for the improvement of conditions for black Americans. But he intended to use moral persuasion rather than guns, for he was already a firm pacifist.

Asa's political beliefs were also influenced by Booker T. Washington and W. E. B. Du Bois, the leading black political theorists of the time. The two men held different views about what blacks should do to better their lives. Washington, the president of an acclaimed black vocational school in Tuskegee, Alabama, stated that black youths should concentrate on getting occupational training and achieving economic self-sufficiency rather than pressing for political or civil rights—an action that would increase racial tensions. His close connections with influential Republican congressmen allowed him to dominate the black political arena and earned him and his group of associates the title of the "Tuskegee Machine."

Du Bois was an outspoken critic of Washington. According to Du Bois, Washington encouraged blacks to accept segregation and other humiliating forms of racial discrimination. A founding member of the NAACP and the editor of the civil rights organization's journal, *The Crisis*, Du Bois advocated a much more radical approach to racial politics. In *The Souls of Black Folk*, a book that he published in 1903, he wrote that blacks should push hard for the overthrow

As a youth, Randolph met the militant AME bishop Henry McNeal Turner at a church convention in Jacksonville. When asked where he found the courage to stand up to southern racists, Turner flourished his Bible and two pistols and said, "My life depends on the will of God and these two guns."

A harsh critic of Booker T. Washington, scholar and editor W. E. B. Du Bois advised bright young black men such as Randolph to get a college education and dedicate themselves to fighting against racial oppression.

of the South's discriminatory voting laws and Jim Crow regulations. He also stated that the finest minds among the black youths should seek college educations, not just the vocational schooling that Washington supported. Du Bois's ideas attracted the support of many young black intellectuals, the group he called the "talented tenth." He believed that these educated young men and women would be the vanguard of a movement to uplift the masses of oppressed black Americans.

Du Bois's arguments impressed Asa and his brother, and they frequently engaged their father in debates about the needs of black Americans. These discussions helped Asa develop his skills in arguing about political and social issues. They also made him long for a wider audience for his views.

When Asa was in his late teens, he spent a summer with a cousin in New York City and worked as a newsboy. Among the musical entertainments he saw there were shows featuring the songs of Rosamond and James Weldon Johnson, two brothers from Jacksonville whose successful songwriting careers in New York had provided inspiration to many hometown boys. Asa's stay in New York gave him a taste for the intellectually stimulating atmosphere of the northern city. Increasingly frustrated by the growing Jim Crow system in Jacksonville and the South, he began to think about making a break from his family and friends.

Finally, in April 1911, having just celebrated his 22nd birthday, Asa decided to leave Jacksonville. He and a friend took jobs as kitchen hands on a New York–bound steamship after telling their parents that they would only be away for the summer. But Asa had no wish ever to return to Jacksonville, and he was determined to put his political beliefs into action and find an outlet for his energy and talents. The budding young social reformer was on his way to a district in New York City called Harlem.

3

HARLEM
FIREBRAND

WHEN RANDOLPH ARRIVED in New York City in the spring of 1911, an area in the northern part of the city was undergoing a transformation. Harlem, whose rows of stately brownstone houses had formerly been the homes of middle-class whites, was attracting an influx of black residents from all over the country. Black real estate agents were buying up large sections of the district following a collapsed real estate boom, and black churches, stores, and social clubs were occupying buildings deserted by whites, who feared being engulfed by the ever-growing body of newcomers.

The white exodus from Harlem was paralleled by a black movement from the southern states to the industrial centers of the North. Desiring a better life than that of an impoverished sharecropper forced to labor under the oppressive weight of the Jim Crow system, blacks were traveling north in search of freedom and economic opportunity. Randolph was part of the first wave of the "Great Migration," the departure of millions of blacks from the South that occurred during the first four decades of the 20th century. In Harlem, he and other southern blacks were joined by native black New Yorkers and im-

After moving to New York City in 1911, Randolph settled in Harlem, a district that was quickly becoming the leading center of black culture and political activism in America.

During the early 1900s, thousands of impoverished black farmers abandoned the tobacco and cotton fields of the South and moved north in search of a better life. Randolph met many of these former southerners in Harlem.

migrants from the West Indian islands. The talents and energies of these different groups gradually combined to make Harlem the political and cultural center of the black American community.

The New York that the 22-year-old Randolph moved to was by no means free of racial discrimination. Blacks were frequently refused service by restaurants and other public facilities, their demands were largely ignored by the city's political bosses, and they were occasionally the targets of mob violence. As in other northern cities where large numbers of blacks were beginning to compete with whites for jobs and housing, racial tensions grew stronger and occasionally erupted into riots.

Randolph's attention was not focused on racial issues following his arrival in New York. After finding cheap lodgings in the center of Harlem, he spent his first months taking in the sights and entertainments of the city and visiting the public library. He was impressed with Harlem and the intense feeling of community spirit and racial pride that he found among its residents. As he said decades later when asked to compare the Harlem of his youth with the Harlem of his old age, "There was a certain standard, social standard, in the life of Negroes in Harlem then. . . . You had a little gloss. There was a deeper sense of respectability with the Negro group. They were trying to do things, trying to achieve status for the race."

Randolph soon discovered that he had to "do things," for he had run out of money and needed to find work. Competition for well-paying jobs was fierce, and he was lucky to find a position as a telephone switchboard operator in a hotel. His first job in New York was followed during the next three years by stints as a dishwasher, floor scrubber, and porter. He also worked as a waiter on a steamship, until he was fired for trying to organize the other waiters to protest against their horrible working conditions.

None of the jobs that Randolph could find were the challenging opportunities that he had come north for or the ones that an educated member of Du Bois's talented tenth of black youth would find acceptable. He adopted the practice of working until he had saved enough money to sustain himself for a while, and then he would quit to pursue his studies and interests.

Randolph had brought with him to New York a firm resolve to participate in the struggle for racial equality, but he was unsure of how to get started. There were few organizations that shared his beliefs in the need for militant social protest or that would welcome a poor, unknown young man into their leadership. In late 1911, he therefore decided to join the Epworth League, a young people's discussion group organized by the Salem Methodist Church in Harlem. The club met once a week to talk about a religious subject, but Randolph usually was able to turn the conversation to political issues. Most of the league

While taking night classes at the City College of New York, Randolph (shown here in 1912) studied the ideas of socialist economic philosopher Karl Marx. Randolph said that his discovery of socialism was "like finally running into an idea which gives you your whole outlook on life."

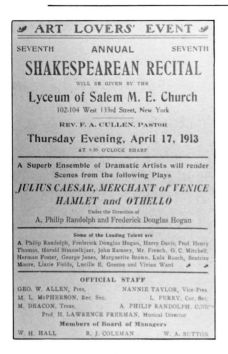

Soon after Randolph arrived in Harlem, he joined a theater group sponsored by the Salem Methodist Church. For a brief period, he considered becoming a professional actor.

members were shocked by his radical political views and considered him a "godless troublemaker," but his impressive debating skills gained him a few enthusiastic supporters.

In addition to participating in the Epworth League's discussion groups, Randolph also joined its drama club and won the lead role in some of the group's theater productions. His outstanding performances drew the attention of Henri Strange, a well-known black actor, who offered Randolph a place in his stage company. Randolph had long dreamed of becoming a professional actor, but after he told his parents about the offer, they wrote back to him stating that they heartily disapproved of their son taking on such a disreputable occupation. Randolph was obedient to their wishes and declined Strange's invitation.

Earlier, Randolph had begun taking a public-speaking course in the evenings at the City College of New York, whose classes were free to all qualified students. With his hopes for an acting career dashed, he turned his full attention to political issues instead. He began attending classes in political science, history, and economics and became a member of City College's debating society. At about the same time, he and some friends from the Epworth Society formed the Independent Political Council, a discussion group that met to debate social and political issues.

While attending City College, Randolph came under the influence of the ideas of the German social theorist Karl Marx and other radical thinkers. Marx wrote that in industrialized countries such as the United States, there was a constant struggle between the huge working class, whose labor provided much of society's wealth, and the relatively small capitalist class, which owned and invested most of the wealth and which exploited the workers. Socialism, the system envisioned by Marx, called for the workers to organize and to seize control of their country's government and industries.

Randolph believed that socialism provided the best means for achieving greater racial equality in America. Because most blacks were members of the working class, they would have much to gain by supporting the socialist movement's labor union activities. However, most labor unions refused to admit blacks into their membership, and Randolph realized that it would be a difficult task to overcome the racial prejudice that stood in the way of unity among American workers.

The City College campus was a hotbed of radical activism. Professors and students frequently held fundraising rallies in support of labor unions such as the International Workers of the World, which was the most militant of the groups that organized strikes to bolster laborers' demands for higher wages and better working conditions. Many of the black students in Randolph's classes shared his enthusiasm for socialism and joined his Independent Political Council discussion group. They began holding public political de-

In 1913, Randolph formed a discussion group called the Independent Political Council and became a radical supporter of the American labor movement. Armed militiamen are shown here confronting a group of striking textile workers.

Randolph first met Lucille Campbell Green, whom he called his "beautiful, gregarious, elegant, fashionable, and socially conscious" wife, at the beauty salon that she owned and operated. The two were married in November 1914 and spent nearly 50 years together.

bates in local churches and soon became known for their radical views. Randolph was the group's leader and its most eloquent spokesman, and he attracted many converts to the socialist cause.

At one of the Independent Political Council debates, Randolph met a young businessman named Ernest Welcome who operated an employment agency called the Brotherhood of Labor. Welcome's agency helped to find jobs for the southern and West Indian blacks who were pouring into Harlem, and it also attempted to teach them what they needed to know to survive and prosper in New York. Impressed by Randolph's well-spoken manner, Welcome hired him to write pamphlets advertising the services offered by the Brotherhood of Labor.

Located in the same building where Welcome had his business was a beauty salon run by Lucille Campbell Green, an attractive widow. Green was a graduate of the hair-styling school operated by Madame C. J. Walker, an enterprising woman who had become a millionaire by marketing hair-straightening products. Walker's splendid house in Harlem served as a gathering place for the elite of black society, and the college-educated and well-to-do Lucille Green frequently attended the parties held there.

After being introduced to Green, Randolph discovered that she shared his interests in socialism and Shakespeare. The 25-year-old part-time student and 31-year-old beautician were immediately attracted to each other. They had a brief courtship, during which they attended many political debates. In November 1914, they were married at the distinguished St. Philip's Episcopal Church in Harlem.

In his marriage to Lucille, Randolph gained a devoted companion who encouraged him to pursue his interests in agitating for social reform. She declared that her beauty salon could support them both, freeing Randolph from the need to work while he continued his studies at City College. A socially committed person herself, the energetic Lucille also worked with a number of community service groups.

Although Randolph and his wife had many interests in common, he avoided the high-society social affairs she attended. Seeing himself as a champion of the black working class, he had little use for the wealthy socialites that were part of Madame Walker's crowd. However, at one of the parties, Lucille met Chandler Owen, a man who seemed to share her husband's radical political beliefs. Owen was a sociology student at nearby Columbia University, and after Lucille introduced him to Randolph, the two young men became nearly inseparable. Randolph greatly admired the brash, irreverent Owen and he enjoyed the free-wheeling debates that they held until late in the night at the Randolphs' apartment on Seventh Avenue in Harlem.

While continuing their studies, Randolph and Owen met at the main public library after classes to discuss how to apply their knowledge about social

Madame C. J. Walker became a millionaire by marketing beauty products such as hair-straightening lotions. She also founded the Lelia College of Hair Culture, where students such as Lucille Green were taught how to use the Walker Company's products.

Impressed by the fiery street-corner orations of socialist speaker Hubert Harrison (shown here), Randolph and his friend Chandler Owen decided to hold daily public debates on the corner of 135th Street and Lenox Avenue in Harlem.

theory to solving America's racial problems. They were constantly going downtown to labor meetings, where speakers such as the Socialist party leader Eugene Debs called for radical reforms that would benefit the workers. They also listened to Harlem street-corner orators, such as the militant socialist Hubert Harrison, urge black workers to demand their fair share of employment opportunities. Inspired by the radical speakers, Randolph and Owen decided to devote themselves full-time to the socialist movement. They quit going to classes, joined the Socialist party, and reshaped the program of the Independent Political Council debating group so that it became even more active in attacking the inequalities in America's economic system.

Taking to the streets of Harlem, Randolph and Owen soon won a reputation as the boldest thinkers among the street-corner orators preaching social reform. Nearly every night, a loud and politically astute crowd gathered at the usual debating spot on the corner of Lenox Avenue and 135th Street to voice their agreement or disapproval of the Randolph and Owen team's speeches. Many of those who listened so intently to Randolph's words were members of the "New Negro" movement, a loose association of militant young intellectuals who were dedicated to lighting the fires of racial pride. Describing Randolph's extreme popularity with Harlem's young political activists, a member of one of his audiences said, "Philip Randolph just seemed to carry the young people in his palms. . . . Instead of rabble rousing, he just talked."

The team's public-speaking abilities brought them to the attention of William White, the president of a black waiters' organization. In January 1917, White asked them to edit a magazine that would deal with topics of interest to waiters working in New York's hotels. Randolph and Owen accepted the offer, which

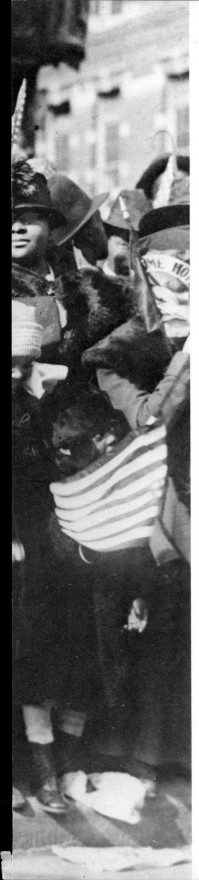

4

THE MESSENGER'S CALL

◆

THE FIRST ISSUE of Randolph and Owens' new monthly magazine reached the newsstands in November 1917. The editors called their publication the *Messenger* and described it as "the first voice of radical, revolutionary, economic and political action among Negroes in America." Priced at 15 cents—a nickel more than other journals at the time—the *Messenger* attracted a small but loyal readership that consisted primarily of young middle-class black intellectuals and white socialists who were interested in racial problems.

Begun with money provided by Lucille Randolph, the *Messenger* had to survive early financial troubles. Neither Randolph nor Owen were interested in the details of running a business, and the magazine's publication date frequently was delayed until the two editors could raise enough funds on lecture tours through northern cities. During its years in print, the magazine twice had to move its Harlem offices after being evicted for nonpayment of rent.

Despite its financial problems, the *Messenger* soon gained a prominent place among New York's political journals. During its early years, the magazine competed with publications such as Hubert Harrison's *Voice*, W. A. Domingo's *Emancipator*, and Cyril Briggs's

During World War I, Randolph and Owen began publishing the Messenger to promote racial pride among blacks. Proud New Yorkers are shown here welcoming home a regiment of black soldiers.

43

Socialist leader Eugene Debs made speeches attacking American participation in World War I. He was sentenced to 10 years in prison for the allegedly subversive antiwar statements that he made in July 1918 at this rally in Canton, Ohio.

Crusader for the ear of the more militant members of the black community. The *Messenger* was considered the most intellectual and controversial of Harlem's radical journals. Randolph's informative, well-reasoned editorials and Owen's more belligerent commentaries made a powerful call for cooperation between workers of all races and for a relentless assault on racism in America. Articles by leading radical thinkers gave insightful reviews about issues of importance to blacks.

The *Messenger*'s first issue appeared at a critical moment in black history. In April 1917, the United States entered World War I, joining Great Britain and France and their allies against the German-Austrian-Turkish alliance. The Germans were often portrayed in American newspapers as being ruthless barbarians, and in his call for national support for the war effort, President Woodrow Wilson insisted that "the world must be made safe for democracy." However, many patriotic citizens disagreed with the decision to go to war and questioned whether the American armies really were fighting to support democratic principles.

Opposition to the war was especially strong among socialists and black radicals. Socialist leaders such as Eugene Debs held rallies around the country and called for an end to a war that they said profited only capitalist arms merchants while killing millions of workers who had been inducted into the armed forces. The U.S. government's response to the antiwar opposition was to pass measures that allowed law officers to crack down on anyone who spoke or published statements against the war. Debs and other vocal dissenters were arrested and sentenced to as many as 10 years in jail.

Blacks generally supported the war, hoping that the benefits of democracy that Wilson talked about would also be extended to themselves. More than 400,000 blacks enlisted in their country's armed forces

and many bought government war bonds. However, the war served to highlight the many grievances of blacks. They were given the lowest-paying and most menial positions in the armed forces and were forced to serve in segregated units. Black regiments were often poorly trained and armed (even so, they still won distinction on many European battlefields).

In the United States, thousands of southern blacks moved to northern cities to take jobs in the arms industries. Crowded into unsanitary slums, hundreds of black workers died at the hands of violent white mobs. Meanwhile, black Americans were asked by their government to lay aside their demands for an improvement in racial conditions so that unity at home could be maintained.

Randolph and other black radicals found it ironic and hypocritical that blacks would be asked to fight for democracy in Europe while being subjected to Jim

Randolph's antiwar speeches and editorials won little support in the black community. The army sergeants shown here were among the 400,000 blacks who enlisted in the American armed forces during World War I.

Randolph and other radical black writers criticized W. E. B. Du Bois for printing an editorial in his magazine, The Crisis, *calling upon blacks to halt their efforts for racial justice and join wholeheartedly in the nation's war effort.*

Crow discrimination and violent mob attacks in their own country. In response to Wilson's call for a democratic crusade abroad, Randolph wrote that blacks "would rather make Georgia safe for the Negro" and that "no intelligent Negro is willing to lay down his life for the United States as it now exists."

The *Messenger* refused to reduce its attacks on the war and America's racial injustices. However, many black publications were willing to obey the U.S. government's prohibitions against printing antiwar literature and criticizing the nation's racial policies. Randolph and Owen were appalled when their old hero W. E. B. Du Bois, the editor of the NAACP's *The Crisis*, called out to the black community to "forget our special grievances and close ranks shoulder to shoulder with our white fellow citizens." Denouncing this viewpoint, Randolph wrote that blacks should be especially forceful in making demands during the wartime when their services as soldiers and workers were especially vital to their country.

Because Randolph and Owen chose to ignore the government's ban on antiwar agitation, they were subjected to extreme harassment. The *Messenger's* offices were invaded; its files and furniture were broken up and scattered. Federal agents kept close surveillance on Randolph and Owen. Finally, the postal department suspended the magazine's second-class mailing privileges, and the editors were forced to use more expensive mail. The Justice Department wanted to prosecute them for treason, but President Wilson feared that such an action would win the two men sympathy in the black community.

Randolph and Owen faced the government pressure squarely and refused to be silenced. They joined other socialist speakers in public demonstrations against the war in cities throughout the country. While they were speaking at a rally in Cleveland, Ohio, a federal agent pulled them from the podium where they were speaking and arrested them. Put on trial for inciting resistance to the U.S. government, Randolph and Owen were amazed when the judge set them free. He refused to believe that the two youthful-looking defendants had written the *Messenger*'s radical editorials, and he advised them to go home to their parents.

Declining the judge's advice, the two editors continued to hold antiwar rallies at black churches and public auditoriums around America. Their tours stopped when Owen was drafted into the army three months before the end of World War I. Randolph was also drafted, in November 1918, but peace was declared shortly before the day that he was to enter. This probably saved him from a long prison sentence. Being a pacifist, he would have refused to serve in the army and would have been subject to prosecution under the nation's strict military draft laws.

During the war years, the *Messenger*'s antiwar position gained little support in the black community. In general, blacks believed they should demonstrate their patriotism and that they would eventually be rewarded for their sacrifices. However, in the period following the war, blacks had reason to question their allegiance to their flag. Fueled by the postwar competition for jobs and housing, racial tensions grew more intense. During the so-called Red Summer of 1919, black communities fought back against rampaging white mobs, sparking off bloody race riots in Chicago and other American cities. A number of black soldiers returning home from the European battlefields were lynched in the South, and dozens of other men and women were murdered by violent white supremacist groups such as the Ku Klux Klan.

During this bitter time, Randolph was full of hope and energy, but he remained convinced that America's racial problems required some drastic solutions. Despite his own pacifist beliefs, he encouraged blacks to use arms if necessary to defend themselves. He

By the middle of 1918, government officials were already calling the Messenger "the most dangerous of all the Negro publications." Randolph said of these times, "We knew we were risking jail, but we didn't give a fig. We were young, we were against everything, and we weren't going to back down from anything."

A cartoon in the September 1919 issue of the Messenger *ridicules the methods that W. E. B. Du Bois (seated) and other black leaders proposed for dealing with America's racial problems.*

wrote that since the nation was unable to protect blacks from lynch mobs and was unwilling to prosecute the murderers, blacks must act according to the accepted law of self-defense: "Always regard your own life as more important than the life of the person about to take yours."

To illustrate its militant message, the *Messenger* printed a bold cartoon showing a white mob fleeing from an armored car driven by a black vigilante. The magazine also printed "If We Must Die," a poem by West Indian writer Claude McKay, which called upon blacks to stand up against their oppressors. The poem's final lines declared:

> Like men we'll face the murderous cowardly pack,
> Pressed to the wall, dying, but fighting back!

As a boy, Randolph had seen his parents take up arms to help prevent a lynching, so his support for militant self-defense measures was understandable. In his editorials, he cited numerous examples to show that the policy was effective. He wrote that white

GIVING THE "HUN" A DOSE OF HIS OWN MEDICINE

LONGVIEW, TEXAS - WASHINGTON, D.C. CHICAGO, ILL. - ?

SINCE THE GOVERNMENT WONT STOP MOB VIOLENCE ILL TAKE A HAND

THE NEW NEGRO

THE "NEW CROWD NEGRO" MAKING AMERICA SAFE FOR HIMSELF

Another cartoon printed in the same issue of the Messenger *shows a black vigilante fighting back against a rampaging white mob. Although a pacifist, Randolph believed that the use of physical force was justified in some instances.*

law officers and town officials in Memphis, Tennessee, had been encouraging an attack on the local black community but had canceled their plans after they discovered that the intended victims were organized and armed. In Longview, Texas, a group of armed defenders killed four men who were trying to lynch a black schoolteacher. The governor of Texas sent the militia to prevent further racial violence even though in the past he had always insisted that state troops could not stop mob attacks.

Few other black leaders shared Randolph's militant spirit. By 1919, he had become outspoken in his criticisms of both past and contemporary black leaders. In his eyes, the men whose ideas he had found so intriguing as a youth in Jacksonville had failed as counselors to their people. He said that although the programs of the late Booker T. Washington and the conservative leaders of the Tuskegee Machine may have helped some blacks get industrial training, their policies encouraged blacks to patiently accept segregation, low wages, and brutal oppression. Randolph

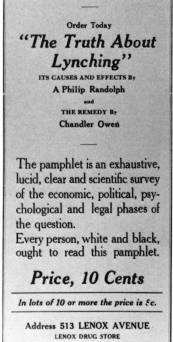

In response to the wave of violent attacks on blacks that occurred after World War I, Randolph and Owen published a pamphlet citing steps blacks should take to prevent lynchings.

criticized Washington's efforts to gain more work for blacks. He said that the *Messenger's* editors "are not interested in Negroes getting more work. Negroes have too much work already. What we want Negroes to get is less work and more wages."

The magazine also wrote hard-hitting editorials against Du Bois and the NAACP, whose staff was composed mainly of liberal white lawyers and other professionals. Randolph wrote that it was impossible for such people to truly understand the needs of working-class blacks.

Randolph's own attempts to win black workers' support for the socialist cause were not very successful. Many people were frightened by the *Messenger's* radical views, and they knew that companies were quick to fire anyone suspected of dealing with union organizers. The U.S. government also exerted pressure on the labor movement. In 1919, Attorney General A. Mitchell Palmer launched an intensive campaign against radical groups, and federal agents arrested thousands of suspected political revolutionaries.

The state of New York decided to conduct a study of local radical groups and appointed a committee headed by State Assemblyman Clayton Lusk to carry out the investigation. Among its other findings, the Lusk Committee stated that the *Messenger* was "the most dangerous of all the Negro publications." The U.S. State Department used this evidence to declare Randolph "the most dangerous Negro in America." However, neither Randolph nor Owen was arrested.

The national campaign against radicals began after Vladimir Lenin's Communist party seized power in Russia and made an appeal to workers around the world to overthrow their country's governments. Like many other radicals, Randolph at first welcomed the Russian Revolution of November 1917, but he was alarmed by many of the communists' beliefs, including their insistence that members must obey the party's rigid political doctrine. By the early 1920s, the *Messenger* was warning black workers against the Communist party's efforts to enlist their support.

Randolph also feuded with the black nationalist leader Marcus Garvey and his Universal Negro Improvement Association (UNIA). A spellbinding orator from Jamaica, Garvey came to the United States in 1916, settled in Harlem, and quickly attracted huge numbers of mainly lower class blacks to his international movement. The UNIA's spectacular, military-style parades and its program of black pride and solidarity appealed to many blacks who saw the race riots of 1919 as evidence that they would never be allowed their full rights as American citizens.

Randolph was initially interested in the UNIA's programs. However, by the early 1920s, the *Messenger* was rebuking Garvey for throwing away the life savings of his poor and uneducated supporters on ill-conceived business ventures such as the UNIA's Black Star steamship company. The rift widened after Garvey admitted to meeting with Ku Klux Klan officials, whom he believed represented the true racial attitudes of white Americans.

Enraged by the UNIA leader's shocking admission of holding such a meeting, Randolph and Owen began a "Garvey Must Go" movement through a political organization they had founded, the Friends of Negro Freedom. The dispute reached a high point when Randolph received a package in the mail containing a human hand and a note warning him not to be a traitor to his race. Randolph suspected that Garvey's organization was involved in the incident. Hostilities between the two men finally cooled after Garvey was imprisoned on a charge of using the mails to defraud the public. The UNIA fell apart after Garvey was deported from the United States in 1927.

One area where Randolph and Garvey differed was in their ideas about how blacks could strengthen their economic positions. The UNIA leader called

During the early 1920s, Randolph engaged in a bitter feud with black nationalist leader Marcus Garvey (shown here). Randolph criticized Garvey for starting poorly planned business ventures with funds raised from the impoverished black working class.

"When you look at Randolph," said one friend, "his rich voice fitted him. It went with everything, even his facial expression, which was one of great dignity." Among his associates, Randolph was known for his sense of humor and as someone who could "calm all tension, anger, and insistent creditors."

on blacks to shun white society and form their own economic institutions. Randolph thought that Garvey's black separatist program was impractical. Instead, he stated that black workers could become a powerful economic force in the United States if they organized and withheld their labor in protest against unfair working conditions. A nationwide strike of black workers could paralyze the American economy and force government and industry to make reforms.

During his years at the *Messenger*, Randolph gained experience in organizing and public speaking. He and Owen campaigned vigorously for Socialist party candidates, and in one New York City mayoral election, they helped turn out more than one-quarter of Harlem's black vote for their candidate. The two men also founded the National Brotherhood Workers of America and a number of other labor associations and political societies. All of the groups soon fell apart, however, and Randolph began to realize that he was a better writer than organizer.

Eventually, Randolph began to see that his efforts to rouse socialist sympathies in Harlem were doomed. Blacks saw no reason to support the labor movement since they were excluded from most labor unions. Randolph wrote many articles criticizing the discriminatory policies of the unions' governing body, the American Federation of Labor (AFL), and its reactionary president, Samuel Gompers. Yet his complaints had little effect. Finally, even Randolph gave up on the Socialist party, discouraged over its neglect of black workers.

By the mid-1920s, Randolph was forced to recognize that times had changed for him and his debt-ridden magazine. The political activism that had marked Harlem during the World War I years was over. During the era of general national prosperity in the 1920s, New York's black intellectuals devoted their energies to the arts, building a celebrated cultural movement that became known as the Harlem Renaissance. The *Messenger* lost its focus as a political journal during this period and became a hodge-podge of articles on art, social commentary, and, as the noted writer Langston Hughes said: "God knows what," a magazine "that reflected the policy of whoever paid best at the time."

Although the *Messenger* struggled on until 1928, its influence had declined considerably. The productive association between the magazine's founders ended in 1923, when Owen moved to Chicago and became a writer for a local newspaper. Randolph received another blow in 1924 when his father died. Paying tribute to the man who had shaped his own militant spirit, Randolph wrote that the reverend represented "that sturdy, stable, old sterling fighting stock of the race and America."

Randolph had few concrete victories to show for the work of his early, radical years other than piles of copies of his once-important magazine. But by 1925, another challenge had been presented to him, and he was turning his attention to the plight of a group of men who worked on America's railroads. ✺

The Messenger *printed notices such as this one calling for cooperation between black and white workers. However, most labor organizations continued to exclude blacks from their membership.*

5

THE
BROTHERHOOD

W HILE WALKING TO his offices one morning
in June 1925, Randolph was met by Ashley Totten,
a Harlem resident who worked as a porter on railroad
sleeping cars. A longtime reader of the *Messenger*,
Totten was well aware of Randolph's commitment to
the struggle of black workers for equal opportunity.
Totten asked the 36-year-old editor if he would speak
to a group of railroad porters on the procedures for
forming a union.

Randolph, whose brother had worked as a porter
a few years earlier, was glad to oblige Totten's request.
The members of his audience were all employees of
the Pullman Company, which owned and operated
the sleeping cars used on long-distance railroad passenger routes. Sleeping-car porters, all of whom were
black, were underpaid and overworked and extremely
unhappy with the Pullman Company, so it is no won-
der that they listened intently to Randolph's discussion of the benefits they could gain by organizing a
strong union.

The porters responded so favorably to Randolph's
ideas that Totten and three other porters—Roy Lan-
caster, Thomas Patterson, and R. R. Matthews—met
with Randolph a few weeks later and asked him to
organize a porters' union. Bound full-time to his magazine and doubtful of his own organizational abilities,
Randolph at first declined the offer. However, after

*Randolph's interest in fostering
black participation in the labor
movement led him to accept the
job of organizing the Brotherhood
of Sleeping Car Porters. Porters
such as the man at left attended
to customers on the Pullman
Company's sleeping cars.*

Although some Pullman porters were highly educated, they were treated like servants who did not even have names. Sleeping car passengers usually called their porters "George," after the company's founder, George Pullman (shown here).

conducting an investigation into the Pullman Company's treatment of its black employees and publishing a series of scathing articles on the subject in the *Messenger*, Randolph changed his mind. He felt committed to helping the porters win their battle.

For almost 60 years, black porters had been providing attentive service to passengers, using the sumptuously furnished sleeping cars first introduced by the entrepreneur George Pullman in the 1860s. The Pullman cars were moving luxury hotels, and it was the porter's job to cater to the passenger's every whim. The porters handled baggage, shined shoes, made beds, and kept the cars spotlessly clean.

In the early years of the Pullman car service, the company mainly employed former slaves, especially men who had worked as household servants on southern plantations before the Civil War. The Pullman Company knew that the former slaves would provide an obedient work force that would take pride in working for a prestigious firm. As the first generation of porters retired, they were increasingly replaced by men with a high school or college education who were were far less willing to accept the slavelike status that the company imposed on its employees.

From the beginning of the Pullman car service, the porters had been paid wages far below the minimum given to white workers with less taxing jobs. In 1919, William McAdoo, the director of the federal railroad administration, ordered the Pullman Company to increase the porters' wages to $60 a month, a still-unacceptable salary. The porters depended on tips received from passengers, which sometimes equaled their monthly wage. However, the tips and wages together amounted to less than two-thirds of the federal standard for minimum acceptable family income.

Living and working out of the large cities where the Pullman Company maintained its stations, the porters were kept constantly on train runs and usually

First introduced to railroad service in the 1860s, the Pullman Company's lavishly decorated sleeping cars offered the ultimate in comfort to passengers traveling between American cities.

When Randolph began to organize the Pullman porters, nearly all of them were black. Overworked and poorly paid, they relied on tips from passengers to earn a living. As one man said, "The best-liked porter is the one who answers his bell before it rings."

were forced to work far more hours than they were actually paid for. Company rules required porters to work 400 hours a month before they could receive overtime pay. In addition, porters were required to pay for their own expenses when waiting for a new assignment away from their home station. Many rarely saw their families.

Unaware of the Pullman porters' working conditions, the general population believed that porters were in a fortunate position. They had job security, a guaranteed wage, an opulent place to work, and the opportunity to travel. Many of the porters saved enough money to buy homes, and they were held in high regard by the black community. However, their status was won at a terrible personal cost.

Backed by the organized labor movement, white railroad workers had formed unions and won wage increases. The Pullman porters had no such protection, and the company had easily smashed all of their past attempts to organize a union. Every porter knew that he would be fired immediately if he spoke out too strongly against his working conditions.

Despite its poor treatment of the porters, the Pullman Company claimed to have a paternalistic concern for the welfare of its workers. In 1924, it organized a company union for the porters called the Plan of Employee Representation. The porters were allowed to choose some of their representatives, but the company's threats and bribes were enough to ensure that its offer of a modest wage increase was approved by the union.

Ashley Totten was one of the porters' representatives in the Plan of Employee Representation. Knowing that a union bound to company management was of little use in negotiating for better conditions and wages, Totten and his associates decided they must have an independent union. They agreed that the editor of the *Messenger* was the ideal candidate for organizing the porters' union. Randolph's deep commitment to unionism was important because the porters knew that they had a long and dangerous struggle ahead of them. The fact that Randolph was not a porter was actually an advantage because he would be less vulnerable to the Pullman Company's threats and tactics to bust a union.

For Randolph, the porters' offer represented a long-sought opportunity to play a leading role in the civil rights movement. He believed that once blacks became a powerful force within organized labor, they could press for greater social equality. In addition, Randolph relished the challenge of helping a group of courageous porters defy the wealthy and arrogant Pullman Company.

In the summer of 1925, porters' union representative Ashley Totten (shown here) began looking for a person "who had the ability and the courage, the stamina and the guts, the manhood and determination of purpose to lead the porters on." He said, "I went to Brother Randolph."

In taking charge of the porters' union, Randolph said, "I consider the fight for the Negro masses the greatest service I can render to my people, and the fight alone is my complete compensation." This cartoon, which was published in the Messenger in 1925, attacks the Pullman Company's exploitation of its employees.

In the summer of 1925, Randolph and the leaders of the New York branch of Pullman porters met to plan their new organization. They decided to call their union the Brotherhood of Sleeping Car Porters. Randolph hoped that the union would gain international recognition and attract members from many nations.

On August 25, at an auditorium in Harlem, the Brotherhood had its first meeting. After cautioning the porters that anything they said would probably be reported back to the Pullman Company by spies in the audience, Randolph proceeded to do all the talking himself. He explained what the Brotherhood would be demanding for the porters: an increase in the minimum wage to $150 a month, a shorter work week, payment for a variety of services that porters usually did for free, and company recognition of the Brotherhood and termination of the Plan of Employee Representation. "Never again," said Randolph, "will Negroes permit white people to select their leaders for them."

The initial response to the Brotherhood was extremely favorable. On the day after the meeting, more than 200 porters signed up for the Brotherhood at its headquarters in the Messenger's offices. Dues collected from union members were enough to get Randolph's organization on its feet. The Brotherhood received additional financial assistance from Randolph's socialist friends and was given a large grant by the Garland Fund, a supporter of liberal causes.

With a modest union treasury established, Randolph began a national tour to organize Brotherhood associations in other parts of the country. Despite the open hostility of the Pullman Company to Randolph's organizing, union branches were soon established in most of the cities where the Pullman stations were located. By the end of 1926, the Brotherhood was claiming a membership of 5,763—more than half of the porters who worked for the Pullman Company.

Milton Webster, who was Randolph's second-in-command and the president of the union's Chicago branch, believed that the porters were bound in Pullman Company chains. He maintained that "the only way that those chains are going to be broken is we have to break them. That is all. There isn't anybody else going to do it for us."

Many dedicated and self-sacrificing men assisted Randolph in building the Brotherhood. One of the first men he met on his tour was Milton Webster, a former porter who had been fired by the Pullman Company for trying to organize a union. Randolph persuaded Webster to organize the Brotherhood branch in his hometown of Chicago, where the Pullman Company had its headquarters and the largest group of porters lived. The hard-nosed Webster was a far better organizer than Randolph and proved to be one of the union's most stalwart leaders.

Among the other Brotherhood organizers who fought courageously to strengthen the union were Benjamin Smith of Omaha, Nebraska; Morris "Dad" Moore and C. L. Dellums of Oakland, California; and E. J. Bradley of St. Louis, Missouri. These and other branch leaders were often singled out for special intimidation by the Pullman Company. Ashley Totten, who served for many years as Randolph's chief assistant, suffered permanent facial damage after being beaten by company thugs.

Confident of its ability to crush an independent porter's union, the Pullman Company at first was scornful of Randolph's organizing efforts. But as the Brotherhood's membership rolls grew larger, the company began a fierce attack on the union. Company officials warned porters not to be seen associating with union organizers or they would be fired. The St. Louis branch of the Brotherhood nearly collapsed after 30 members were dismissed. "The Pullman Company will never recognize Randolph, and there's nothing he can do about it," said a Pullman official to one group of porters. Claiming that the United States was "a white man's country," the official swore that his company would never "sit down around the same table with Randolph as long as he's black."

The Pullman Company also attempted to destroy the standing of Randolph and the Brotherhood in the black community. Letters distributed by the company portrayed Randolph as a dangerous radical who was determined to destroy the livelihoods of a group of misguided porters. The attacks were effective in dividing the black community. The NAACP and the National Urban League both backed the Brotherhood, and they were joined by a few church leaders and other prominent citizens. However, most ministers and community leaders were, as Milton Webster termed it, "cowarded" by the Pullman Company's threats to stop using blacks as porters. The black press was also generally hostile to Randolph—an attitude that was probably due in part to the fact that the Pullman Company placed well-paying advertisements in newspapers that criticized the union.

There were also differences of opinion among the Brotherhood's leadership. Webster wanted the union to begin striking and picketing to win immediate wage concessions. Randolph, on the other hand, believed that the Brotherhood should work for the greater goal of building a labor and civil rights movement. He said this could only be accomplished by fighting for changes in national labor laws, and he proposed that the Brotherhood hire lawyers and lobbyists and put pressure on federal administrators and congressmen. Webster and Randolph often quarreled about the tactics the union should use, but they were bound together by their common cause and the deep respect they felt for each other.

The Brotherhood survived the well-organized smear campaign waged against Randolph by the Pullman Company and hostile black newspapers. Within a year of the union's founding, Randolph's campaign to win legal recognition for his organization was well under way. First, he persuaded Emanuel Celler, a congressman from New York, to introduce a bill in the House of Representatives calling for an investigation of the Pullman Company's labor practices. This effort was unsuccessful, but Randolph soon turned his attention to the Railway Labor Act of 1926. The

By the end of 1926, the Brotherhood had established branches in most large American cities. Randolph (fourth from right) is shown here at a union meeting with a group of associates that includes Benjamin Smith (second from left) and Ashley Totten (second from right).

The Brotherhood of Sleeping Car Porters
STANDS FOR SERVICE NOT SERVITUDE

LIGHTING THE WAY TO OUR RACE'S ECONOMIC INDEPENDENCE

Randolph aroused a spirit of great self-sacrifice among the Brotherhood's members. "It was like a light," one porter said after hearing Randolph speak. "From that day on I was determined that I was gonna fight for freedom."

newly passed federal law provided for the establishment of a board of commissioners that could be used to settle any disputes between management and employees that might lead to a disruption in railway service. Among its other duties, the mediation board was supposed to ensure that a company did not try to intimidate employee representatives.

Randolph decided that the Railway Labor Act could be used to force the Pullman Company to negotiate with the Brotherhood. During the fall of 1926, he wrote letters to the company's officials requesting that they meet with him to discuss the porters' demands. The company simply ignored the letters. Randolph then wrote to the railroad mediation board and asked it to intercede in the dispute between the Brotherhood and the Pullman Company. The board acknowledged Randolph's request and appointed Edward Morrow, the former governor of Kentucky, to investigate the dispute.

To prepare the Brotherhood's case, Randolph hired a team of labor lawyers and researchers. Although the fees for the work cut deeply into the union treasury, Randolph was armed with detailed figures and a well-written legal argument when he arrived at the initial inquiry in December 1926. However, the Pullman Company had its own figures, which showed that 85 percent of the porters supported the company's Plan of Employee Representation. The company told Morrow that Randolph had no right to say that he represented the majority of the porters. Randolph disputed the Pullman Company's claims and submitted written evidence showing that management officials had threatened to fire any employee who did not support the company union.

After hearing the cases on both sides, Morrow adjourned the meeting while he studied the evidence. The inquiry was reconvened in July 1927, but by then

Following the passage of the Railway Labor Act of 1926, Randolph requested that the federal government intervene in the dispute between the Brotherhood and the Pullman Company. He is shown here meeting with Edward Morrow of the railroad mediation board.

STRIKE NOTICE

To All Pullman Porters and Maids

On account of the refusal of the Pullman Company to settle the dispute on Recognition of Wages and Rules governing Working Conditions with the Brotherhood of Sleeping Car Porters, a strike has been declared and shall be enforced on all Pullman Cars effective

FRIDAY, JUNE 8th
12 O'clock Noon

For further information call Glendale 6373. You are requested to attend the meetings to be held each evening from 4 until 6 o'clock at **2382 18th street.**

BENNIE SMITH
Field Organizer

By Order of Strike Committee

In July 1927, after the Pullman Company broke off negotiations with the Brotherhood, Randolph began organizing support for a porters' strike. The union set a date of June 8, 1928.

the Pullman Company had decided that it would have nothing more to do with the proceedings. Company representatives wrote to Morrow that there was no dispute between management and employees and that there was no need for further discussion. Morrow had to end the inquiry since he had no power to force the company to attend the meeting.

The termination of the talks was a huge blow to the morale of the Brotherhood's members, but Randolph was not defeated. "The fight has just begun," he announced as he made preparations to force the company to resume negotiations. There was one more weapon to use. If the railroad's mediation board believed that the porters were about to go on strike, it could request that the Pullman Company agree to have the dispute settled by arbitration.

The Brotherhood's organizers began to rouse support for a strike. Randolph traveled to Chicago and other centers of union activity and spoke to the porters about why their leaders felt that it was necessary to take a gamble that would endanger the lives and jobs of the Brotherhood's members. The men listened to the eloquent, dignified man they called "Chief" with a mixture of awe and reverence. Randolph was able to convince many of them that their future well-being was at stake. In May 1928, he announced that the porters were prepared to go on strike.

Further discussions between the Brotherhood and Pullman officials were held, but no progress was made. The Pullman Company had decided that the Brotherhood was bluffing. The mediation board did not believe the porters would strike and refused to order emergency arbitration. Faced with the necessity of having to order the strike to begin, Randolph had to back down. He knew that his union did not have the financial resources to engage the Pullman Company in an open battle. If the Brotherhood called for a strike, there would be massive firings and many of the picketers would be thrown in jail. Randolph was unwilling to make the porters choose between their jobs and their union.

In July 1928, the mediation board dropped the Brotherhood's case, declaring that no further discussion was necessary. Having relied on the provisions of the Railway Labor Act, Randolph was disappointed to learn that the mediation board had been holding secret discussions with the Pullman Company. His faith in the American legal system was severely shaken by the news.

For Randolph, the summer of 1928 was an extremely painful time. His brother, who had been taking college courses in New York, had died of diphtheria a few months earlier. The extreme grief he felt over James's death was compounded by his feeling of having failed the porters. There seemed to be no way to break the Pullman Company's stranglehold on their powerless black workers.

The Brotherhood had experienced a bitter setback, but Randolph held on to his dreams of building a strong black labor movement. A year before, he had said that the fight had just begun. Recent events had proved that the struggle would be a long one, but he was still confident that patience would be rewarded and justice would come. ◆

"We thought Randolph (shown here) was crazy," band leader Noble Sissle said of the labor leader. "You going to fight the Pullman Company? You going to unionize the Pullman porter? Randolph going to fight Pullman's millions of dollars when half the time he didn't have a dime in his pocket?"

6

COLLECTIVE DIGNITY

———— ❧ ————

IN THE WAKE of the Brotherhood's defeat in the 1928 showdown with the Pullman Company, Randolph knew that steps had to be taken to shore up the porters' confidence in their union. The union must demonstrate, he said, "that we are on a solid foundation and that we are here to stay."

In 1929, the Brotherhood held a national convention in Chicago, at which delegates from the different branches met to write a constitution and choose officers. Randolph was elected president, and Webster was named vice-president. However, the convention did little to halt the drop in the union's membership.

With the union's treasury almost depleted, Randolph was confronted with the pressing need to raise funds. Public benefits helped to bring in some money, and more funds were solicited through advertisments in the union's news bulletin, the *Black Worker*. Although hard-pressed to meet business expenses, Randolph refused contributions from other unions and liberal white organizations. He stated that black workers must "pay the price and bear the brunt of their own struggle." The porters' cause, he said, was one battle that blacks would have to win on their own.

Not everyone understood Randolph's high ideals. To many of the Brotherhood's members, the union's objectives seemed to be slipping farther away. The

With slogans such as "Fight or Be Slaves" and "Never Say Die," Randolph and the Brotherhood loyalists vowed to continue the struggle for true union representation.

Pullman Company continued to harass its employees and force them to accept intolerable working conditions. The company had succeeded in freezing out the porters' union. But Randolph was confident that as long as the Brotherhood survived, there was hope.

In an effort to increase the Brotherhood's prestige and give it more weight in dealing with the Pullman Company, Randolph applied for membership in the American Federation of Labor. His first application in 1926 had been rejected due to a technicality. With the encouragement of AFL president William Green, who sympathized with the Brotherhood's cause, Randolph made a second application, which was accepted in 1929. However, because the porters' union did not have enough members or funds to satisfy AFL standards, it was not given the full status as an international union that Randolph had requested.

Although the American Federation of Labor (AFL) had a long history of racial discrimination, Randolph believed that the organization could be persuaded to assist black workers. AFL members are shown here at a convention in the 1890s.

Radical black groups such as the communist American Negro Labor Congress harshly criticized the Brotherhood's leaders for joining a racist organization like the AFL. Randolph acknowledged the truth of their statements about the federation. In the past, he himself had attacked the AFL's racist policies and had called it the "American Separation of Labor." However, he believed that black workers must have representatives in the most powerful labor federation in the country. As Webster said in response to the criticisms of the Brotherhood's entry into the AFL, "In America, if we should stay out of everything that's prejudiced we wouldn't be in anything."

Randolph intended that his toehold in the AFL would become "the spearhead which will make possible the organization of Negro workers." He believed that the Brotherhood had to be the conscience of the labor movement, and he intended to use the hammer of moral persuasion to change the racist policies of the AFL unions. In the resolutions that he presented to the federation's executive board, he called for fully integrated unions. He argued that only an alliance of black and white workers would allow the labor movement to achieve its goal of raising the living standards of American workers. With the workers divided by racial barriers, it was all too easy for employers to hire blacks as strikebreakers to undercut the power of the unions.

Despite Randolph's best efforts, the Brotherhood's membership continued to decline. The situation grew especially grim during the early 1930s after a worldwide economic depression brought hard times to millions of people. Amid the poverty, unemployment, and despair that followed in the wake of the depression, interest in the activities of the porters' union was further diminished. By the beginning of 1933, the Brotherhood's dues-paying membership had sunk to one-tenth of its 1926 strength. Most people thought that the union had long since passed away.

In 1929, AFL president William Green approved Randolph's request that the Brotherhood be allowed to join America's largest labor federation.

When President Franklin Roosevelt entered office in January 1933, the country was in the midst of a deep economic depression. His New Deal programs included measures that required companies to negotiate with labor unions.

During this period, the Brotherhood was nearly bankrupt. Some of the men who had been fired from their porter jobs and then spent years of labor in the union's service were starving and homeless. Members who had managed to put away some savings tried to help their beleaguered brothers, but few had any money. Although Randolph and a skeleton staff continued to issue reports and make recruiting drives, there were almost no funds left for union business. Randolph carried on with his plans, bearing with equanimity the fact that most black leaders shunned him.

Matters became worse after the Brotherhood was evicted from the building in which it had its New York headquarters and was forced to move to a small apartment. The adversity inspired the remaining staff members to acts of great self-sacrifice. They lived on bread and milk to ensure that there was money to mail business letters and to send Randolph to labor conferences.

Randolph himself was in desperate circumstances. Lucille's beauty salon had folded, and they had to live on his $10-a-week union salary. Friends bought them food to keep them going. When Randolph traveled on business, he wore the same suit and pair of socks throughout the trip because he had no other presentable clothes. His associates were embarrassed to see him wearing patched-up rags, but he appeared not to notice. Despite his impoverished condition, he rejected a good job with the New York government that was offered to him by a longtime friend, Mayor Fiorello La Guardia. He felt he had to finish his job with the porters, and he was still hoping and struggling for a better day. "Nothing can keep us from winning," he insisted.

The Brotherhood's situation began to improve after Franklin D. Roosevelt was elected president in 1932 and announced his plans for a program to restore national prosperity, which he called the New Deal. The recovery program included public works projects, social relief measures, and reform legislation that put thousands of unemployed people back to work and provided money to local governments to help those who had been devastated by the depression.

Roosevelt's administration was committed to correcting weaknesses in federal labor laws. Many railroad employees associations had complained that the Railway Labor Act did little to protect workers from being exploited by their companies. The Brotherhood and other unions cheered in June 1933 after Congress passed two laws that strengthened the position of railroad workers, the Emergency Railroad Transportation Act (ERTA) and the National Industrial Recovery Act (NIRA). Section 7a of the NIRA guaranteed laborers in the railroad and certain other industries the right to organize, select representatives of their own free choice, and bargain with their company as a collective group.

Randolph's joy over the passage of the ERTA and NIRA quickly died. The guidelines of the new laws classified the Pullman Company not as a railroad passenger company but rather as a hotel service, and the legislation did not cover hotel workers. Outraged by this ruling, Randolph wrote letters of protest to Roosevelt and sympathetic congressmen. He also pressured the leaders of other railroad unions to demand that the Brotherhood be included in the new labor laws. In 1934, after a strong effort by Senator Clarence Dill of Washington to change the ERTA, the act was amended and the Pullman Company was listed as a railroad company.

The new ruling was a tremendous boost to Randolph and the Brotherhood, but the battle for union recognition was not yet won. The Pullman Company refused to talk with Randolph and began laying off porters it suspected of being sympathetic to the Brotherhood. However, at Randolph's request, the railroad mediation board ordered an election be held to choose new employee representatives for the Pullman por-

Brotherhood organizer C. L. Dellums said that the tall, thin Randolph "was my idea of a revolutionary leader. I had never heard of a fat one yet. I figured the fat ones must worry about their bellies too much."

ters. A secret ballot was used to ensure that the company could not intimidate its workers. On June 27, 1935, the results of the election were announced, and the Brotherhood had won by a margin of more than six to one. Cheering the good news, the black magazine *Opportunity* proclaimed, "No labor leadership in America has faced greater odds. None has won a greater victory."

Collective bargaining negotiations between the Brotherhood and the Pullman Company began soon after the election. On July 29, 1935, a proud group of union representatives, which included Randolph, Webster, Benjamin Smith, C. L. Dellums, E. J. Bradley, Thomas Patterson, and Clarence Kendrick, marched into the Pullman headquarters in Chicago. They sat down at a table across from the officers of a company that had sworn never to deal on an equal basis with a group of black porters.

The negotiations began slowly and dragged on for month after month. The Pullman Company continually delayed discussions, hoping that the porters' support for the Brotherhood would collapse if no quick

Celebratory rallies were held in black communities throughout the country in June 1935 after the Brotherhood won the right to represent the Pullman porters. Randolph sent a telegram to the NAACP exulting, "First victory of Negro workers over great industrial corporation."

agreement was reached. This tactic achieved nothing, so the company reportedly offered Randolph a huge bribe to desert the union. But as Brotherhood officer Dellums said of Randolph, "You couldn't get him to abandon his principles. He is the only man I know that nothing could buy."

Eventually, the Pullman Company began to bargain in earnest. Randolph's associates were tough and intimidating-looking men who easily held their own when discussions broke down into screaming and cursing matches. However, none had any knowledge of negotiating tactics. They depended on Randolph to interpret the complex language used by company lawyers. As one delegate said, "None of us was prepared, none had any special training, none really educated. But here we were around this wonderful man."

Randolph kept pounding away at the Pullman Company. On August 25, 1937, the 12th anniversary of the founding of the Brotherhood, the Pullman representatives signed an agreement that gave the porters the wage and work-hour concessions that the union had demanded. The long, bitter fight was over.

On August 25, 1937, the Pullman Company gave the porters a huge wage increase. The union representatives who negotiated the settlement included (left to right) L. O. Manson, Benjamin Smith, Ashley Totten, Thomas Patterson, Randolph, Milton Webster, C. L. Dellums, and E. J. Bradley.

Randolph's stunning triumph over the Pullman Company elevated him to national prominence. Porters such as the one shown here formed a band of highly motivated Brotherhood members that Randolph could rely on to agitate for the rights of black workers.

Randolph's faith in America's legislative system and legal processes had finally been rewarded. As he would say later, "In our struggle to build the union we faced destitution and continual harassment, but we did build it, and our struggle conferred upon us collectively a certain dignity."

The Brotherhood's victory brought Randolph into the national limelight. A virtual outcast only a few years before, he was now recognized as one of the most capable and influential leaders in the black community and American labor movement. He was deluged with requests to give addresses at important social functions, and people once more greeted him when he walked on the streets of Harlem. Meanwhile, the increase in dues-paying members helped improve the Brotherhood's financial position.

Randolph's success in the Pullman porters' struggle helped give new impetus to the national campaign for civil rights reforms. In February 1936, more than 800 representatives from black associations met in Chicago to form the National Negro Congress, an agency that would devote itself to assisting black groups in the battle against discrimination.

Although Randolph was ill and could not attend the first meeting of the National Negro Congress, the body's executive board nonetheless selected him to be the president of the association. He gladly accepted the position, excited by the opportunity to lead, as he called it, "a united front of all Negro organizations."

During Randolph's term in office, he worked hard to promote the cause of black workers. He also warned about the threat that the racist, expansionist regime of the German dictator Adolf Hitler posed to peace and democracy in Europe and the rest of the world. Randolph took little part in the congress's daily operations, but he used his position to draw public attention to the racial inequalities that continued to plague America's economic system.

The National Negro Congress never grew into the active, broad-based organization that Randolph hoped it would become. Moreover, the increasingly influential role played by black communist members in the congress's affairs worried Randolph. He resigned the presidency at the 1940 national convention after the delegates voted to support the communists' programs.

Throughout the 1930s, Randolph continued his battle against racism in the labor movement. After 1936, when the Brotherhood of Sleeping Car Porters

From 1937 to 1940, Randolph was president of a coalition of civil rights organizations called the National Negro Congress. He is shown here addressing delegates at one of the congress's annual conventions.

During the 1930s, United Mine Workers' president John L. Lewis (shown here) was one of the few labor leaders who supported Randolph's efforts to form an alliance between black and white workers.

was finally granted full status in the AFL, he was in a somewhat better position to pressure the federation to make reforms. The AFL's president, William Green, was unwilling to give strong support to the Brotherhood's campaign efforts against union racism, but Randolph found allies in John L. Lewis of the United Mine Workers and David Dubinsky of the International Ladies Garment Workers Union. Lewis's and Dubinsky's unions were racially integrated, and both men believed that blacks must be allowed greater participation in labor associations.

In the mid-1930s, Lewis led an exodus from the AFL by a group of unions that wanted workers to be organized according to the industry in which they were employed rather than by the particular job they held. They believed, for instance, that engineers, conductors, and porters should all be represented by one railroad workers' union. Although Randolph shared this belief, he decided to keep the Brotherhood in the AFL rather than join Lewis's new labor federation, the Congress of Industrial Organizations (CIO). The AFL remained the most most powerful workers' organization in America, and Randolph decided that he could accomplish more for blacks by trying to reform the racially biased unions in the AFL than in joining the relatively liberal unions in the CIO.

Year after year, Randolph continued his lonely battle to integrate the AFL unions. At every annual AFL meeting, he and Milton Webster issued resolutions calling on the federation to make a greater effort to organize black workers and to expel any unions that excluded blacks and other nonwhite groups from their membership. The resolutions always met with a generally hostile response, and Randolph often was subjected to vicious name-calling and accusations that he was trying to destroy the labor movement. Randolph endured the insults with serene dignity and even took a little pride in the fact that some of his

The unions that split off from the AFL in the mid-1930s to form the Congress of Industrial Organizations (CIO) were generally more open to black members than was the AFL. However, Randolph chose to remain in the AFL and continue his battle to integrate all of the federation's unions.

colleagues believed he was a former university professor and that he was trying to intimidate them with his "Harvard accent."

The struggle for racial equality in the labor movement made only limited progress during Randolph's first two decades as a representative in the AFL. But by bringing the issue into the open, he forced the AFL unions to confront their own racism and to understand its harmful effect on the labor movement. Looking back on his and Webster's trying times in the AFL, Randolph would later say, "We gave them hell every year. They didn't pass our resolutions, but we brought them religion." The Brotherhood's preacher would eventually win over his converts.

7

"LET THE NEGRO MASSES SPEAK"

LATE IN 1940, Randolph and Milton Webster were conducting a railroad tour of the Brotherhood of Sleeping Car Porters' branches in the South. Looking out the train window at sharecroppers' cabins and other evidences of black poverty caused by the Jim Crow system, the 51-year-old Randolph began to think hard about how he could stir up effective action against racial discrimination using the same methods of nonviolent protest employed by Mahatma Gandhi in India. Suddenly, he had a brainstorm. Turning to Webster, he said, "I think we ought to get 10,000 Negroes to march on Washington in protest—march down Pennsylvania Avenue. What do you think of that?"

Considering the huge public-relations and organizational problems involved in bringing thousands of people from different walks of life together for a rally in the nation's capital, most black leaders would have decided that it was a totally unmanageable idea. But to Randolph, the difficulties seemed small in comparison to the urgent problems facing black Americans. He believed that the moment was right for an action that would electrify the black community and gain the attention of the nation's leaders.

During the 1940s, Randolph waged an intensive campaign to eliminate racial discrimination in America's industries and armed forces. He is shown at left picketing outside the site of the Democratic National Convention in 1948.

At the time, America was preparing for its eventual entry into World War II. In Europe, Great Britain was being hard-pressed to hold off the conquering armies of Germany and Italy, while in the East, Japan had gained control of much of eastern Asia. American industry was gearing up to produce arms for the war effort, and large amounts of weapons and supplies were already being sent to the British. A nation preoccupied with the talk of war hardly seemed the best place to organize a civil rights movement.

Whereas in 1918 Randolph had protested against America's participation in World War I, in 1940, he supported a war against Adolf Hitler's Nazi regime. However, he retained his old belief that during war-

Many new jobs were created in the American defense industries in the early 1940s, but most companies maintained their policy of hiring blacks only for the most menial positions.

time blacks should exert extra pressure on the government to make social reforms. He did not think that such protests were unpatriotic. Rather, he insisted that while blacks were doing their best to serve their country, it was the duty of all patriotic Americans to ensure that none of their fellow citizens were discriminated against on racial grounds.

Discrimination was still deeply rooted in the American economy. Although the defense industry's increased production created thousands of jobs and helped to restore the nation's economic health following the Great Depression, blacks did not share in the new prosperity. In 1940, there were only 240 blacks among the 100,000 employees of the aircraft industry, and most of them were janitors. The defense industry plants suffered from extreme labor shortages, but because of companies' discriminatory hiring policies, more than a half million skilled black workers were idle. The living standards of most blacks actually declined, but in a terrible irony, the federal government reduced its public relief programs because it believed they were no longer vital.

It was easy for Randolph to find clear-cut examples of discrimination. In a public statement about its employment policies, one aircraft manufacturing company said that although it was "in complete sympathy" with blacks, it would not hire them as production workers or mechanics. "There will be some jobs as janitors for Negroes," the company added. The federal government made no effort to ensure that the corporations it did business with had fair employment practices. In fact, the government condoned discrimination in its own agencies.

The situation was hardly better within the nation's armed forces. In the army, black soldiers were kept in segregated units and had little chance of being promoted to officers. Once they completed their training, they were usually assigned to manual labor units. In the navy, blacks were used as cooks and

Secretary of War Henry Stimson's statement that leadership qualities are not "embedded in the Negro race" was typical of the prejudiced beliefs held by many high government officials.

stewards, while they were not allowed into the air force or marines at all. As a final indignity, black soldiers were at first rejected as blood donors by the army, and even after they were accepted, their plasma was kept separate from that of white donors.

One sign that the armed forces' racially discriminatory policies might be changing occurred in October 1940, when Benjamin O. Davis, one of the few high-ranking black officers in the army, was promoted to brigadier general. However, Henry Stimson, the secretary of the War Department (later renamed the Defense Department), stated that the army would remain segregated and that the black combat troop units would be commanded by white officers. In defense of the practice of not promoting blacks to higher positions, Stimson said, "Leadership is not imbedded in the Negro race yet."

Leadership was a quality that Randolph knew a great deal about. In September 1940, at a Brotherhood convention, he issued a resolution calling for an end to discrimination in the armed forces. Among the guests at the convention was President Roosevelt's wife, Eleanor, a staunch supporter of civil rights reforms. The First Lady's response to the resolution was to arrange a conference at the White House to discuss the grievances of the black community.

On September 27, 1940, Roosevelt and key administration officials met with Randolph, Walter White of the NAACP, and T. Arnold Hill of the National Urban League. At the meeting, the three black leaders asked for the immediate integration of the armed services, and they believed that their request was well received.

However, the Roosevelt administration was afraid that an order barring racial discrimination would upset southern congressmen and their constituents, and it was unwilling to make changes. The White House's press release on the meeting stated that the military's segregation policy had been approved by Randolph, White, and Hill. The three men were outraged by the false statement, and it was only with difficulty that they were able to clear their names before the black community. In attempting to atone for the error by his staff member, Roosevelt sent a letter of apology to the three men. He stated that some reforms would be made in the military's policies toward blacks but that segregation would remain in effect.

In the face of the continuing, blatant racism at all levels of American society, Randolph concluded that the time was right for direct action. During a train ride in 1940 with Webster, he decided that his next mission would be to lead a huge protest rally in the nation's capital. The demonstration would harness the anger of America's oppressed black citizens and turn it into a positive display of solidarity and force. Randolph sensed the great potential political

Randolph's efforts to persuade the Roosevelt administration to order equal treatment for black servicemen met with little success. The men shown here are members of a segregated army engineer battalion.

"We loyal Negro American citizens demand the right to work and fight for our country," became the slogan of Randolph's March on Washington Committee (MOWC) after he declared his intention of leading a massive protest rally in the nation's capital. Some groups picketed local defense companies to show their support for the march.

power in the black masses. He knew that if he could unite the various groups in the black community, Roosevelt would have to listen to their demands.

In January 1941, Randolph announced that he was organizing a march to "shake up America." He said that the "leaders in Washington will never give the Negro justice until they see masses—10, 20, 50 thousand Negroes on the White House Lawn!" The objective of the march, which was scheduled for July 1, 1941, would be to force integration in the military and win employment opportunities for blacks in the defense industry. Randolph stressed that blacks were merely demanding the right to serve their country.

The response was instantaneous. People from around the country wrote to Randolph at the Brotherhood's headquarters in New York requesting information on how they could participate in the march.

A large group of prominent ministers, organization directors, and union leaders joined Randolph in forming a March on Washington Committee (MOWC) to coordinate the demonstration. He also employed his network of porters to rouse support for the march. However, his most effective tool in drumming up interest in the movement was the prestige of his own name.

In March 1941, Randolph issued a statement about the goals and principles of the MOWC. He wrote, "In this period of power politics, nothing counts but pressure, more pressure, and still more pressure." A massive, nonviolent demonstration of black unity in Washington, D.C., he stated, could force Roosevelt to issue an executive order banning the types of discrimination that the marchers would be protesting against. The march would culminate in a rally at the Lincoln Memorial, and Eleanor Roosevelt and a number of administration officials would be invited to address the crowd.

Randolph's campaign to "shake up America" enjoyed such strong popularity that bookstores were named after the proposed march.

Randolph received some criticism over his rule that only blacks would be allowed to participate in the march. "There are some things Negroes must do alone," he said, calling on white sympathizers to cheer the marchers on from the sidelines. Blacks must win this crusade for self-respect by themselves.

Randolph opened two offices in New York, and with the support of the black press, enthusiasm for the march was roused throughout the country. Black fraternal organizations, labor unions, church groups, and women's clubs responded by holding benefits to raise the money needed to transport themselves to Washington in July.

Randolph once again began speaking on the streets of Harlem. He visited pool halls, beauty parlors, bars, restaurants, and barbershops and talked about the plans for the march. His spirits were high, his optimism was infectious, and his energy was astonishing. Crowds gathered around him to hear his call to action, "Let the Negro masses speak!" By May, he was asking for 100,000 people to march on Washington.

As the day of the march grew nearer and support for the movement continued to grow, the Roosevelt administration became increasingly upset at the idea of thousands of black demonstrators descending on the capital. Seeking to make some amends to black workers, federal officials sent a letter to defense industry companies asking them to make a greater effort to hire blacks. Randolph was not impressed, and he said that the president must issue an executive order "with teeth in it."

In refusing Roosevelt's appeal to call off the march while committees were formed to study the black labor problem, Randolph said that "the hearts of Negroes are greatly disturbed and their eyes and hopes are centered on this March." He invited Roosevelt to address the rally as the guardian of the American democracy.

In desperation, Roosevelt asked his wife and Mayor La Guardia of New York to talk to Randolph and persuade him to call off the march. Randolph was not convinced by his two friends' arguments that the march might lead to a backlash that would produce even worse conditions for blacks.

Finally, Roosevelt invited Randolph to the White House for further discussions. At the meeting on June 18, 1941, the president learned that he could not persuade Randolph to stop the march without an executive order. Relenting at last, Roosevelt said that he would make the necessary decree.

The president's staff went through numerous drafts of the executive order before they wrote one that satisfied Randolph. During the ordeal, one staff member burst out, "Who the hell is this guy Randolph? What the hell has he got over the president of the United States?" The answer was that Randolph was the revered leader of a powerful black coalition.

New York mayor Fiorello La Guardia (right) and First Lady Eleanor Roosevelt were unable to persuade their friend Randolph to cancel the demonstration in Washington, D.C. In June 1941, President Roosevelt finally issued an order ending discrimination in the defense industries.

After renaming his committee the March on Washington Movement, Randolph organized a series of rallies to rouse black solidarity. Members of the organization's planning committee are shown here discussing preparations for the 1942 Madison Square Garden rally.

On June 25, 1941, Roosevelt issued Executive Order 8802, which declared that racially discriminatory employment policies in the defense industry and federal goverment were illegal. The order also established the Fair Employment Practices Committee (FEPC) to investigate complaints of discrimination and arrange steps to correct grievances.

On a radio broadcast on June 28, Randolph told his supporters that the battle had been won and that he was calling off the march. Some of the younger, more militant members of the MOWC protested the decision and said that they wanted a visible show of black strength. However, Randolph pointed out that the movement's main goals had been met and that the weapons of organized black power and direct action must not be used lightly. He agreed, though, that the MOWC's work was far from finished. For instance, although blacks were being accepted into the marines and air force, they were still serving in segregated units throughout the military.

Randolph vowed to keep on pressing for equal rights. MOWC was renamed the March on Washington Movement (MOWM), indicating a broader effort and an ongoing commitment to social reform. Randolph knew that the organization would have to keep a close watch over the FEPC to make sure that rules were being followed. To generate continued enthusiasm for the MOWM cause, Randolph staged three tremendous rallies in New York, Chicago, and St. Louis.

The efforts of Randolph and the MOWM led to dramatic gains by black workers. After the United States entered World War II in December 1941, there was a greater demand for black labor. By the end of the war, blacks composed more than eight percent of the defense industry's work force. Many of them were welcomed into the more liberal unions in the CIO labor federation. Through the FEPC, the federal government was drawn into the battle for an integrated workplace.

In 1942, Randolph's service to the black community was recognized when he was awarded the prestigious Spingarn Medal. That same year, Randolph was named an advisor to a newly formed civil rights group, the Congress of Racial Equality (CORE). At the organization's annual convention in 1943, he called upon the assembled delegates to use only nonviolent means in protesting their country's racial injustices.

By the summer of 1943, much of the momentum of the MOWM was gone. The war absorbed much of the nation's energy, and many blacks felt satisfied that progress was being made on civil rights measures.

Yet Randolph still found many matters that disturbed him. His continuing efforts to eliminate racism in the AFL met with staunch resistance. In July 1943, Roosevelt moved the FEPC under the jurisdiction of

An outbreak of racial disturbances in the summer of 1943 proved that tensions between blacks and whites remained high in spite of Randolph's calls for interracial cooperation. Men arrested during a riot in Harlem are shown here being driven to prison.

the War Manpower Commission, an agency that was not sympathetic to blacks. Black soldiers being trained in army camps in the South were frequently harassed by local white communities.

In the summer of 1943, racial tensions erupted into bloody race riots in cities and army camps throughout the nation. There was little further progress in the civil rights movement during the war. In April 1945, as the fighting in Europe was coming to an end, the country mourned the death of Roosevelt. The president was succeeded by Harry S. Truman, who was in office when Japan surrendered in August 1945, ending World War II.

During the war, Randolph and other black leaders were never content with the armed forces' racial policies. In 1947, after Truman called for a peacetime draft that would require all men of military age to register, Randolph saw an opportunity for pressure and reform. Because the president's new draft bill did not mention racial integration of the armed forces,

Randolph and a New York state official named Grant Reynolds formed the League for Nonviolent Civil Disobedience Against Military Segregation. Randolph chose a radical socialist and CORE member, Bayard Rustin, to direct the organization.

Again, Randolph prepared to hold demonstrations and declared that his group would be satisfied with nothing less than a presidential order. In March 1948, worried that another march was in the making, Truman held a meeting with Randolph, Walter White, educator Mary McLeod Bethune, Lester Granger of the National Urban League, and Charles Houston of the NAACP. Randolph was by now an old hand at handling pressure from the White House. Neither he nor Truman budged from their positions.

Later that month, Randolph and Reynolds began a civil disobedience campaign that included advising and urging young black men not to register for the draft. Called before the Senate Armed Services Committee to discuss the military's racial policies, Randolph and Reynolds made it clear that they would continue their resistance to segregated armed forces. Stating that he was governed by "a higher law than any passed by a national legislature in an era when racism spells our doom," Randolph vowed that he would be willing to go to jail for his convictions.

In July 1948, Randolph and other protesters picketed outside the Democratic National Convention headquarters in Philadelphia, Pennsylvania. The pressure was effective. Truman needed the support of blacks to win the presidential election in November, and so he issued two executive orders. One created a Fair Employment Board whose task would be to eliminate racial discrimination in government agencies. The second executive order established a committee to begin the desegregation of the armed forces.

By the time he reached the age of 60, Randolph had done a great deal to help blacks gain equal rights. Yet there were more achievements to come. ◆◇◆

Bayard Rustin (shown here) was among the young black militants of MOWC who criticized Randolph for calling off the march after forcing Roosevelt to issue an executive order. Rustin later became Randolph's chief associate.

8

THE ELDER STATESMAN

·❦·

ALTHOUGH RANDOLPH WAS in his sixties when the 1950s began, he had no thoughts of retiring from the field of battle. With the honor and prestige he had reaped from his many successful past endeavors, he was in a good position to affect the forces that were changing America.

By the 1950s, the labor movement had finally begun to accept the principles that Randolph had been championing. Other union leaders grudgingly accorded him their respect, and he was chosen as a delegate to international labor conventions. After the AFL and CIO merged in 1955, he was elected to the federation's executive council, and he helped organize a committee on civil rights affairs to study the effects of racism in labor unions. In 1957, Randolph received an even greater honor when he was elected vice-president of the federation.

Most of the unions in the AFL-CIO were racially integrated by the late 1950s. However, Randolph was still not satisfied with this; his attempts to wipe out the last vestiges of racism within the federation led to many stormy sessions in the executive council. In 1959, he was censured by the council for making

On August 28, 1963, more than 200,000 people gathered in Washington, D.C., to join Randolph's March for Jobs and Freedom. He is shown here at far right in the front row of the marchers.

95

During the 1950s, many labor unions granted full membership rights to black workers. Elected vice-president of the AFL-CIO in 1957, Randolph also appeared as a union delegate at international labor conferences such as this one in Milan, Italy.

public complaints that the AFL-CIO was not doing enough for black union members. At the time, an angry George Meany, William Green's successor as AFL president, yelled at Randolph, "Who the hell appointed you the guardian of the Negro members in America?"

Meany soon came to realize that Randolph did indeed represent most of the nation's black workers. The two men settled their differences, and Meany became Randolph's greatest ally in the labor movement. During the 1960s, the AFL-CIO was a strong supporter of civil rights legislation.

Randolph worked with many different labor groups. In 1960, he helped to form the Negro American Labor Council, an organization that worked to increase the role of blacks in labor unions; he served as president of the council until 1966. In 1964, with funding from the AFL-CIO, he founded the A. Philip Randolph Institute, an organization committed to eliminating discriminatory hiring practices and lobbying for a wide range of social programs for the needy.

Randolph's work during the 1940s not only led to labor reforms but also helped to foster a powerful civil rights movement in the following decade. The struggle for racial equality changed its focus in the 1950s, shifting away from the campaigns for presidential orders that Randolph had waged earlier. Increasingly, black groups targeted the Supreme Court and Congress, hoping to win judicial decrees and federal laws to bolster their cause. In 1954, the Supreme Court ruled in the case of *Brown* v. *Board of Education of Topeka* that segregation in public schools was illegal, and civil rights organizations stepped up efforts to integrate the nation's educational system.

The South, where most of the worst cases of racial oppression existed, was the main battleground for the civil rights struggle. Many different forms of protest were used against southern Jim Crow practices. Black students held sit-ins at whites-only restaurant lunch counters. Communities boycotted bus services that discriminated against black passengers. Protest marches against segregation were held in Birmingham and Montgomery, Alabama, and in other cities. The struggle was by no means easy. Civil rights demonstrations sparked off violent resistance from conservative white southerners. The nation recoiled in horror as black churches were bombed, police turned high-pressure water hoses on children marching in demonstrations, and civil rights workers were kidnapped and murdered.

During these years of racial protest, Randolph was no longer the chief spokesman for black Americans. Other leaders had emerged to take the reins of com-

The Reverend Ralph Abernathy was one of the most prominent leaders of the civil rights movement in the 1950s. He is shown here speaking at his church in Montgomery, Alabama, during the black community's boycott of the city's bus services in February 1956.

mand in the racial struggle. They included James Farmer of CORE, Martin Luther King, Jr., Ralph Abernathy, and Fred Shuttlesworth of the Southern Christian Leadership Conference, John Lewis and Stokely Carmichael of the Student Nonviolent Coordinating Committee (SNCC), Roy Wilkins of the NAACP, and Elijah Muhammad and Malcolm X of the Black Muslim movement. Most of these men had been heavily influenced by Randolph's pioneering protest work. His success in gaining greater opportunities for black workers had opened the way for a broadening of the civil rights struggle.

The leaders of the various black groups often held strongly conflicting views, and some were bitter enemies. Randolph was the one man who could bring them all together and win their support for new civil rights campaigns. He treated everyone with respect and was in turn viewed as a kind of wise, benevolent father figure by the younger leaders. The friendly relationship between him and King, the most influential black leader of the period, was especially important to the success of the movement.

During the late 1950s, Randolph was once again busy organizing marches. In Washington, D.C., in 1957, he led the largest civil rights march up to that time, a demonstration called the Prayer Pilgrimage. In 1958, he returned to the capital and was joined by baseball star Jackie Robinson and actor Harry Belafonte in leading 10,000 students in the Youth March for Integrated Schools. During this period, thousands of people from all over the world visited Randolph in his Harlem office to seek his advice in leading reform movements in their own countries.

In many of his efforts, Randolph was assisted by Bayard Rustin, the director of the A. Philip Randolph Institute. The two had a close association. More than 20 years younger than Randolph, Rustin had a long and distinguished record in the civil rights movement. In 1947, he and a group of other CORE members had boarded an interstate bus reserved for whites, beginning the first of the "freedom rides" against the Jim Crow system.

Early in 1963, Randolph issued his call for a march on Washington to draw national attention to the need for civil rights legislation. The organizer of the huge demonstration was Randolph's longtime associate Bayard Rustin, shown here making an address after the march.

Even as he entered his seventh decade, Randolph maintained the same upright bearing. His friend C. L. Dellums said he was "just as straight as if there was a board in his back." His gentle, patient manner had not changed either. In describing Randolph's demeanor, journalist Murray Kempton said that many of his opponents were "driven to outsized rages by the shock that anyone so polite could cling so stubbornly to what he believes."

Throughout his years of struggle, Randolph was lucky to have his "Buddy," the nickname he and his wife used for each other. He was utterly devoted to Lucille and helped nurse her through her final years when she was crippled by arthritis. They never had children, thus Randolph was left alone after Lucille died on April 12, 1963.

The continuous pressure exerted by black groups gradually led to a more receptive climate for civil rights legislation in the early 1960s. John F. Kennedy became president and stated his support for a broad agenda of social reforms. With the black New York congressman Adam Clayton Powell, Jr., sitting as chairman of the House of Representatives' Labor and Education Committee, progress was made on a series of proposals for civil rights measures, including bills requiring nondiscriminatory labor practices.

Randolph believed that a massive demonstration was still needed to build national support for civil rights action. Early in 1963, he announced his plans to hold a rally he called the March for Jobs and Freedom. He said that the march would be held in Washington on August 28, 1963, and that Bayard Rustin would be the organizer.

As in 1940, the enthusiasm for an assembly that would unite civil rights supporters from around the nation was overwhelming. The task of arranging services for the marchers was a daunting assignment. Rustin did a heroic job of coordinating the march preparations from a small office in Harlem.

Not everyone was certain that the march was a good idea. President Kennedy was concerned that the demonstration might turn violent and that the proposed civil rights legislation in Congress would be endangered by any unfortunate displays. He had a meeting with Randolph, King, and a group of other black leaders to express his reservations about what would happen if blacks started holding massive street demonstrations. "Mr. President, the Negroes are already in the street," said Randolph, cautioning the chief executive that it was better if leaders committed to nonviolent protest led the demonstrations. Kennedy agreed and gave his blessing to the march.

The day finally arrived, and more than 200,000 people gathered in the capital for the march to the Lincoln Memorial. The march was entirely peaceful

"Let the nation and the world know the meaning of our numbers," Randolph said in his opening speech at the rally that followed the 1963 march on Washington.

and presented the nation with an awesome display celebrating love for freedom and human dignity. Randolph gave the inaugural address to the people gathered at the Lincoln Memorial. The march, he said, "is not the climax of our struggle but a new beginning." As the crowd roared its approval, he added, "Let the nation and the world know the meaning of our numbers. . . . We are the advance guard of a massive moral revolution for jobs and freedom."

At the conclusion of the rally, Randolph presented Martin Luther King, Jr., who told the crowds, "I have a dream today." King's grand vision, the exuberance of the crowd, and the recitals of hauntingly beautiful spirituals deeply moved the normally reserved Randolph. Tears streamed down his face as the ceremony ended and the marchers prepared to return home.

In the wake of the march came a great tragedy. President Kennedy was assassinated in Dallas, Texas, in November 1963. The civil rights legislation that the president had called for was enacted under his

In September 1964, President Johnson awarded the Medal of Freedom to Randolph for his services to his country. Among Randolph's many achievements was his call for a march on Washington, which he termed "an outcry for freedom, for justice."

successor, Lyndon Johnson. Randolph's work in bringing about a more equitable America was recognized in 1964 when Johnson presented him with the Medal of Freedom, the nation's highest award for civilians.

The new laws did not end resistance to civil rights programs. In some areas where Jim Crow practices were strongly enforced, little progress was made. The Ku Klux Klan and other white supremacist groups reacted to the new laws with a campaign of violence. Pressed beyond their limit by the wave of beatings and lynchings, some civil rights groups such as the SNCC foreswore their former policy of nonviolence and called for armed retaliation. U.S. participation in the unpopular Vietnam War increased the feelings of unrest. Martin Luther King, Jr.'s assassination in April 1968 let loose a fury of destructive rage that resulted in race riots in cities throughout the country.

Randolph was saddened that the civil rights movement's earlier spirit of peace and goodwill seemed to have been swept away. But remembering his own response in the *Messenger* to racial violence that occurred 50 years before, he could well understand the anger and frustration felt by the Black Panthers and other militant black groups. Nevertheless, he continued to counsel black activists that they should rely on peaceful means of protest. "Victims of great oppression, youngsters who have dreams for a better future, they remind me of my own self in the '20s," he said. He counseled black youths to educate themselves and not get left behind by the dizzying pace of technological change. Slogans such as "Black Power," he said, were no substitute for positive action to achieve civil rights reforms.

To many of the young radicals of the 1960s, Randolph's calls for nonviolent demonstrations seemed old-fashioned. Some told him he should retire and leave the fighting to leaders who were willing to use the barrel of a gun to make a political statement. But

Commenting about the victories of the civil rights movement in the early 1960s, Randolph said, "Freedom is never granted; it is won. Justice is never given; it is exacted." President Lyndon Johnson is shown here with Martin Luther King, Jr., after signing the Civil Rights Act of 1964.

Coretta Scott King (center) and AFL-CIO president George Meaney (left) were among 1,300 of Randolph's friends who gathered on April 15, 1969, to celebrate his 80th birthday.

others honored him. One of Randolph's young admirers said, "He was a radical at a time when it meant loss of life. . . . He has given us the opportunity to shout out loud, 'I'm black and I'm proud.' "

In 1968, still bearing his tall, straight carriage, Randolph attended his last meeting as president of the Brotherhood of Sleeping Car Porters. While resigning the job that he had held for 43 years, he thanked the men who had been his comrades through the times of extreme hardship. By this time, the union's heyday had long since passed, but Randolph could look back with pride upon the important role the Brotherhood had played in national affairs.

On April 15, 1969, 1,300 of Randolph's friends gathered at the Waldorf-Astoria Hotel in New York to celebrate his 80th birthday. During the toasts to Randolph, Bayard Rustin described him as a man who never had a bad word to say about anyone. Coretta Scott King, the widow of Martin Luther King, Jr., thanked him for being such a wonderful inspiration to her husband.

During the last decade of his life, Randolph continued to inspire people. Labor leaders pointed to him as their guiding spirit and used his tactics of nonviolent mass protest to organize demonstrations. The A. Philip Randolph Institute carried on its important work of making sure that Randolph's ideals were not forgotten.

Randolph died on May 16, 1979, a few weeks after his 90th birthday. He left behind him a life of courage and dignity. He also left millions of friends and disciples. Roy Wilkins, in describing Randolph's influence on him, said:

> You caught me at a time when every young college boy should be caught—when he is full of idealism and when he believes that the world can be changed. And here was a man changing it, who was confident it could be changed, who never faltered, who never gave his followers anything but the hope of victory.

Against immense odds, Randolph won victories that helped to unleash the winds of change across America. He proved time and time again that human dignity and the rights of ordinary citizens are more important than a company's property and profits. As a messenger of peace and social justice, he helped to form a brotherhood of all free and courageous people and led it on a march for a better world. Randolph called the 1963 march on Washington a new beginning; if his ideals and principles continue to be followed, America will benefit from many more triumphs of the human spirit like the ones engineered by A. Philip Randolph. ❧

"It is part of the greatness of A. Philip Randolph," said Bayard Rustin, that he "maintained a total vision of the goal of freedom for his people as well as of the means by which it must be achieved."

CHRONOLOGY

———— ❧ ————

April 15, 1889	Born Asa Philip Randolph in Crescent City, Florida
1903	Enters the Cookman Institute in Jacksonville, Florida
1907	Graduates from the Cookman Institute
1911	Arrives in Harlem, New York
1914	Marries Lucille Campbell Green
1917	Begins to publish the *Messenger*
1925	Organizes the Brotherhood of Sleeping Car Porters union
1936	Elected president of the National Negro Congress; the Brotherhood is accepted as a full member of the American Federation of Labor
1937	The Pullman Company signs agreement with the Brotherhood
1940	Randolph resigns as the president of the National Negro Congress
1941	Announces the organization of the March on Washington Committee
1942	Awarded the Spingarn Medal; named as adviser to the Congress of Racial Equality
1943	Stages a demonstration at Madison Square Garden in New York City
1955	Elected to the AFL-CIO's executive council
1957	Elected vice-president of the AFL-CIO
1960	Helps to form the Negro American Labor Council
1963	Wife, Lucille, dies; Randolph helps to lead the March on Washington
1964	Founds the A. Philip Randolph Institute with funds from the AFL-CIO; presented with the Presidential Medal of Freedom
May 16, 1979	Randolph dies

FURTHER READING

Adams, Julius. *The Challenge: A Study in Negro Leadership*. New York: W. Malliet, 1949.

Anderson, Jervis. *A. Philip Randolph: A Biographical Portrait*. New York: Harcourt Brace Jovanovich, 1972.

———. *The Meaning of Our Numbers*. New York: Harcourt Brace Jovanovich, 1972.

A. Philip Randolph at 80: Tributes and Recollections. Excerpts from speeches made at the 80th birthday dinner, May 6, 1969, Waldorf Astoria Hotel, New York City. A. Philip Randolph Institute.

Blum, John Morton. *V Was for Victory: Politics and American Culture During World War II*. New York: Harcourt Brace Jovanovich, 1976.

Embree, Edwin R. *Thirteen Against the Odds*. New York: Viking, 1944.

Garfinkel, Herbert. *When Negroes March: The March on Washington Movement in the Organizational Politics for FEPC*. New York: Atheneum, 1969.

Harris, William. *Keeping the Faith: A. Philip Randolph, Milton P. Webster, and the Brotherhood of Sleeping Car Porters, 1925–1937*. Champaign, IL: University of Illinois Press, 1977.

Meier, August, Elliott Rudwick, Francis L. Broderick, eds. *Black Protest Thought in the Twentieth Century*. 2 ed. Indianapolis, IN: Bobbs-Merrill, 1971.

Polenberg, Richard. *War and Society: The United States 1941–1945*. Westport, CT: Greenwood, 1972.

INDEX

PICTURE CREDITS

————————— ❦ —————————

SALLY HANLEY was born in Chicago, Illinois, and educated at the University of Wisconsin and the University of Bridgeport before receiving a Ph.D. from Lehigh University. She is currently chairman of the Department of History at Franklin College in Indiana.

NATHAN IRVIN HUGGINS is W.E.B. Du Bois Professor of History and Director of the W.E.B. Du Bois Institute for Afro-American Research at Harvard University. He previously taught at Columbia University. Professor Huggins is the author of numerous books, including *Black Odyssey: The Afro-American Ordeal in Slavery*, *The Harlem Renaissance*, and *Slave and Citizen: The Life of Frederick Douglass*.